UNDERR8TED

THE ROUTE THAT CAUGHT AN NFL DREAM

Wallace Miles

DEDICATION

This book is dedicated to my grandmother Mary Julia Wynn, who taught me peace in all storms. To my grandfather Roy Wynn Sr. who hovered around just in case I strayed too close to the water before I was ready. To my beloved Aunt Julia Mae Wallace, who carried me to my field of dreams. And, to my namesake, my Uncle Wallace Garfield Miles, whom I never had the privilege to meet but I have felt with me my entire life. I love and miss you all.

ACKNOWLEDGMENTS

There is no me without all those who have poured into me my entire life. I am forever grateful to all those who have touched my life. To my parents Annette Wynn and Marvin Miles, who created a nurturing space of support, opportunity, and growth, I am eternally grateful. I carry you into every interaction, every opportunity, every challenge, and every triumph.

TESTIMONIALS

"Some people are motivated, while others are driven. Motivation comes and goes, but being driven is a trait that's innate and will last forever. Wallace Miles is an individual that is driven in every aspect of life. There are few people in this world who truly inspire me. Wallace Miles is on that list."

- Milt Stegall (CFL Hall of Famer)

"The first thing I noticed about Wallace wasn't his ability; it was his effort and "want to." Wallace did not settle for good enough. He wanted to be the best, so he just outworked everyone. He enjoys the process. He likes the work. The more you threw at him, the harder he worked.

What I admired most about Wallace is that he did things the right way. He led by example and got the most out of himself and his teammates.

Wallace got better every time he touched the field and I believe he carried that on throughout his football career."

- Doug Brown

TABLE OF CONTENTS

OVERTIME

EPILOGUE

5

INTRODUCTION

"HARD WORK ON THREE! ONE... TWO... THREE... HARD WORK!" As we huddled for the last time at rookie minicamp, I couldn't believe where I was. Standing on an NFL field, a place I had dreamed about since I was four years old. Surrounded by 50 other guys who were standing in the midst of their version of the same dream, the ambiance intensified. Though we all worked so hard to get here, we all were approaching a pivotal point in our lives that was no longer in our control. Pride and joy came face to face with fear and doubt, creating a toiling of emotion within me. There was nothing more I could do, but hope I was enough.

As we all started walking to the sidelines, heading to the locker room, my eyes jumped around to see how my peers were reacting to this moment. Some were stoic, seemingly unfazed by the moment. There were some joking and playing around, either oblivious to what was about to happen or confident in their position. Lastly, there were those that were like me, conscious of the enormity of the situation with concern stamped all over their faces.

As I continued to scan my surroundings, my eyes came across a set of eyes that seemed to be looking right back at me. The doubt swirling within said: "He is looking past you." The owner of this set of eyes started walking toward me with a smile on his face. The doubt continued to whisper, "He's going to talk to someone else!" But as our paths reached a connecting point, he stopped right in front of me. The owner of that set of eyes was Chris Trotter, the General Manager of the Detroit Lions. He told me I had a good camp, and that I showed a lot over the last three days. Overtaken by the moment, I managed to respond, "Thank you, I appreciate the opportunity." Then he told me something that almost broke me down on the spot. I never knew how impactful words could be, or how much emotion they could trigger until this moment. Every second I had spent on a field practicing, watching film, in a gym lifting weights, or in my bed dreaming a dream, had all brought me to this moment. Mr. Trotter said, "WE'RE GOING TO SIGN YOU!"

We all have a story. We all are here for each other. This book is written about me for you. To help you create your journey. No matter where we start in life, we can grow from what we learn. When you feel what is meant for you, make your decision, make your move, get off your release, get out of your break, and go like it's the only life you have. As we break this huddle and get set for this journey, sit back, relax, tie up your shoelaces, and buckle your chin strap, because it's going to be a bumpy ride.

FOREWORD

UNDERR8TED: *The Route That Caught an NFL Dream* is a true American story about a boy's journey through uncertainty to gain what his four-year-old self saw as success. {Through every trial and tribulation, you are about to read about, you will gain insight into what it takes to become an NFL receiver on a road less traveled. The author also presents tools for everyone to use to become successful in any and every aspect of their own life.} The constant evolution of this true story makes the reader stop and think about how they approach their own life. Am I this passionate about what I do? What am I prioritizing? Am I working hard enough to accomplish my goals? Have I given this life everything I have to offer?

Given that Wallace J Miles is my oldest friend, I am inclined to provide a bit more context into the mind that created UNDERR8TED and verify a few events coming up. I'll take on the latter first. The book's subtitle gives away the fact that Wallace accomplishes his dream of making it to the NFL. Yes, he signed an NFL contract. I watched him play on ESPN many times and traveled to watch him play in person professionally. Yes, he was the high-school kicker and barely touched the field as a wide receiver. While most future college and NFL players dominate high school football he was relegated to kicking. He hints at this but, in a football locker room the kicker is often an afterthought and not considered a part of the team.

During his struggle with just being the kicker I personally called him, "Kicker slash Wide Receiver". I always stated kicker first. My intent was to motivate him. Although, we would not become close until later when we played soccer together our senior year of high school, anyone around Wallace could tell there was a fire in him to play receiver that could not be contained. Anyone could also see he loathed being the kicker. I can still tell kicking is and will always be an afterthought as he never mentions in this book that he kicked multiple field goals and extra points as a kicker in college. This just further emphasizes your true passions always shine through. Yes, he missed an important practice for a dentist appointment. To be fair the appointment was needed. Yes, he ran great routes and made multiple big plays in his last high school game.

After that game, a couple of underclassmen asked our wide receiver coach about Wallace and all the coach could do was shake his head. He didn't have any words. I knew then that the team had wasted Wallace's receiving talent by forcing him to just focus on kicking. Yes, he walked on as a backup kicker at North Carolina A&T State University. For those not familiar with the walk-on situation,

Wallace was accepted into A&T purely on his test scores and academic accomplishments. He always believed that the way to the field was first through the classroom. Once he was accepted, the football program had no risk in allowing him to attend practice as a kicker. The most they would lose is the five minutes he took to take practice kicks. The football program could cut him from the team at any time.

Yes, he committed his full self to football and school his freshman year. Yes, he became the star receiver for his college and was put back on the scout team for being late to church. Funny enough, I drove four and half hours to watch him play that game that he hardly got into. Even more ironic, it was one of the games that aired on ESPN. When we caught it replaying on ESPN U later that night, Wallace was highlighted as one of the two players to watch. At some point in the second half of the game the ESPN announcer wondered, where was Wallace Miles? Yes, he went from being a walk-on kicker to a leader on the team. Yes, he graduated college with an Electrical Engineering Degree. And yes, there is so much more you will learn as you go along this journey with him.

Now to the former. A couple of my own thoughts on Wallace's mindset to keep in mind while reading this book. In the summer of 2019, I asked Wallace to play in a "pickup" community kickball game with people playing with age ranges from 7 to 55. By the end of the game, Wallace was kicking the ball over everyone's head. He was picking up the kid running in front of him so they both could score, and his team would win. He is extremely competitive!

In high-school after I beat Wallace in Madden, I went to use the bathroom in his childhood home. I saw a sticky note on his bathroom mirror. It listed how much he wanted to squat and bench. His expected GPA for the year and socially how he wanted to become more outgoing. He accomplished them all. The day before Wallace's wedding a groomsman asked his father what was the key to happiness in life? Without hesitation he affirmed, "Figure out what you want and make it happen." Whether you agree with that affirmation or not, Wallace has an innate ability to figure out what he wants and somehow do it. Most of this book is the how he went from "I want to be a receiver" to running routes for an NFL team.

While I had a firsthand account of this story, I still found myself fascinated by it. I am still taken aback at times by how an individual with so little pedigree and countless pitfalls was able to accomplish so much. The author would say, "Every setback is a setup to a major comeback!" After reading this book even the most skeptical person will have hope.

If you are looking for motivation, you have stumbled across a book full of it. Wallace would also always say, "Everyone has their own story. It's up to them what the story says". After you finish reading this book, go out and create your own story. Learn from every occurrence and grow beyond those limits you thought you had.

Foreword by: James Hicks

WARMUPS

CHAPTER 1 - WHO AM I

52 years ago, Wallace Garfield Miles was shot and killed in the streets of Baltimore, Maryland by a coward. At 19 years old the presence of Wallace Miles, his opportunities, and his life were all taken away. Not only were they taken away from him, but also taken away from his family specifically his younger brother Marvin Miles. Marvin and his older brother Wallace were extremely close. They loved each other as brothers should. They fought each other as rivals, competed against each other, and then loved each other again all in the same day.

POPS

Marvin, who became my father named me after his brother and best friend Wallace Miles. In my family this name means something. There is a weight to it. As I later learned, I inherited a responsibility that comes with that name. I could not waste the second chance for the name Wallace Miles to live. From that tragedy came life.

I came into this world under fairly normal circumstances. I have been blessed to have both parents there to shower me with love and family to do the same. I was the third child to my father and first to my mother.

My Father was born and raised in those same murderous, drug infested streets that claimed the life of his brother. He is the second of four children. Despite tragedy striking so close to his heart, he kept his head held high. He was able to maneuver his way through the streets of Baltimore and ultimately to Morgan State University. There he joined the football team as an UNDERR8TED walk on. He fought and competed with the best of them until duty called. His future wife found out she was pregnant with my older brother, Marvin Miles Jr, and later my older sister Kimberly.

Carrying the new responsibility of being a father to his newborn son he left the game he loved and disenrolled from Morgan State to pursue work. His next move was enlisting in the Air Force to serve his country and provide for his new family. Somehow, even with this detour he pressed forward and eventually graduated from Troy State University with a degree in Accounting. His perseverance in the wake of tragedy and the adversities life presented to him, set in motion a new standard for his family. He set the tone of overcoming for all who followed to pull from. He walked into the dreams of generations before him because he did not just accept what life presented him. He decided there was more. He decided he wanted more. He decided he was going to have more.

MOM DUKES

On the other side of me, is my mother, who has had to overcome countless social, gender, racial, and economic barriers. She was born in the tiny rural town of Sparta, GA. A town that still carries the remnants of the culture of slavery. Segregation and Jim Crow laws were prominent, with sharecropping being the only consistent means of employment. Though she was too young, her sibling worked in the fields picking cotton and other agriculture. The spirit of the old south was alive. Neither her mother nor her father made it to high school, because education was not as valued as survival was.

At the age of 5, she was subject to a major change of scenery. Her family moved from the backwoods of Georgia to the mean, grimy streets of Philadelphia, PA for the promise of better work opportunities. Though financial prosperity never found them, family support anchored them during this transition. That support helped my mother to carry the baton from her parents and older siblings. She carried it first through high school and later to graduating from college. She attended "The" Howard University as an UNDERR8TED walk on to the volleyball team. Using the survival skills instilled in her by her family, she earned a scholarship and graduated with her degree in Architectural Engineering. She has always broken barriers and is quietly

16

trailblazing a path for all those that follow. She understood how essential education was and the opportunities it opens. Overcoming the remnants of slavery and driving forward, first on the shoulders of her family, and then lifting off and flying with her own wings. She has shown her family what the Wright brothers showed the world, that we can fly.

TEAMWORK

By the time I came around, my parents had decent occupations in what was considered a meager economy. We were considered a lower, middle-class family, but class didn't mean anything to a child engulfed in love. There was a roof over our heads, food on our tables, and a bed to lay in regardless of anything else we had to sacrifice. Pops was up before the sun like clockwork. As I look back on it, I'm not sure how he did it. Before I could finish wiping the crust out of my eyes, he had my clothes ready, his work bag packed, food on the table, and the car was outside warming up.

His heroics didn't end with just being faster than the sun or causing the most important meal of the day to materialize on a plate in front of me. After his long days at work, he would pick me up from school and race me to the car. In my eyes, he was like the Flash. I could never beat him, no matter how much of a head start I took. When we would get home after basketball, soccer, or baseball practice, he had the strength to go over my homework. The freakish thing about it was he mustered the strength to do this 365 days a year and 366 on leap years. Rain, sleet, sunshine, tired, or sick, it didn't matter, you could count on him. Superman is a cartoon. I could introduce you to a real one.

Mom is her own version of a superhero. I didn't understand her true sacrifice until I was older, but she was my guardian angel, up for any battle. She woke up every morning and went to work in a different world. It was filled with people who neither looked like her nor wanted her to be there. Being black in the engineering and construction field presents daily adversity, but to be a black woman caused an entirely different riff on her path. She could probably spend an entire month telling you every hardship and injustice she endured for being born a black woman who loved what she did. It wasn't until college that I ever really knew her struggles. That's the kind of woman she is. Stress from work, marriage, family, and the community rained down on her in monsoons. All I saw was her handling her business with love and care. No matter what the day gave her she still came home with all of it in one arm. She cooked dinner, bathed us, helped us with our homework and did our hair. I used to have a "Dynomite" afro that she would turn into Allen Iverson braids.

When I was little, she would massage my muscles to make sure I was always ready to hit the ground running. After all of her daily heroics, she had the nerve to read us a bedtime story to ease our minds as we drifted into Never Never Land! As we slept, she would pray a cloak of protection over us. She is logical, ethical, and spiritual. She is our prayer warrior. She taught us to treat all people with love and respect. Her standards were high above the clouds, but she has always been there as the wind beneath our wings. Everything she touches flourishes, as if she carried the light of the sun. My dreams are possible because of her sacrifices, her selflessness, her prayer, and her support.

The union of these two resilient people produced me and my younger sister, Claudia. They brought me home to the Metropolitan community of Atlanta, Ga. A place riddled with drugs, prostitution, and crime. This was not what my parents wanted me to see when I hopped off the porch as a child. They put a plan in place that created the opportunity for us to get out. They bought some land in a quiet South Atlanta suburb, right outside of the city. There they built a home for our family to grow.

As a unit they always wanted to protect us physically, mentally, and what we would later learn, spiritually. They showed us what love was. They showed us what support and belief looked like. No matter how tired or frustrated they may have been, their effort to show us unconditional love was limitless.

Somehow as a black youth in America, I became hooked on soccer of all things. We played just about every weekend. In all the games I played in, I can't recall a single game where I didn't have at least one parent at the field to cheer me on. They always made me feel like I was a priority. This is the key in any relationship that unlocks the full potential of the connection. For a child, it's almost essential to life because it's instinctive to want to do things for the approval of our guardians. Children want to feel loved and relevant in the eyes of those they look up to. This love and support fortifies the mind of a child. If you don't feel that you have that kind of support from the guidance in your life, maybe that person does not know what it looks or sounds like. You as the youth may have to take the lead and express to them that you want their support. Tell them it would mean the world to you, to have them cheering, guiding, and coaching from your corner. Sometimes the follower must aid in the leadership. Sometimes the follower must become the leader. All of our stories are different, but all of us need love and support, especially in our youth. Thank you, Mom! Thank you, Dad! You did exactly what you were supposed to do and more.

So, who is Wallace Miles? He is the product of all that came before him. A culmination of all the sacrifices, triumphs, and tragedies two families have absorbed. Between being named after my uncle and being the seed of two people who broke through the concrete to sprout their petals, a "WHY" was instilled in me at an early age. My life represented opportunity. From the tragedy of death, I had the opportunity to represent my uncle in this world. My life represents the dream that so many slaves dreamt but could never attain. My parents overcame societal adversity to take steps beyond those their parents could reach. It's my "WHY" to continue the progression of a people and the progression of my family.

What is your why? What grounds you and drives you at the same time? What source is going to get you through the days you don't feel like it? What "why" is going to get you out of bed when sleep feels so good? What "why" is going to be in your corner after you have been beat down by the game? What whispers in your ear to get back in the ring because you've got more to give? Before you turn this page, state your why, write it down, and feel the power it gives you!

You thought I was playing. Go find a pen. I'll wait.

MY WHY IS:

_____

_____

_____

_____

_____

FIRST QUARTER

CHAPTER 2 – THE BEGINNING

Running onto the field after we scored a touchdown, the nerves began shaking my body. Stepping to the holder, Joe, our backup quarterback, and a good friend of mine, I showed him where I wanted him to place the ball. I took my customary three steps back and two steps to the left, followed by my signature foot twist, signifying I was digging in and ready. I gave Joe a nod and he started the cadence. "Blue 18, Blue 18, Set....!" The center snapped the ball.

Ideally, the snapper is supposed to snap the ball directly to the hands of the holder. The holder then catches it and places it on the spot that I, the kicker, had designated. Then it's on the kicker to connect his foot with the ball, sending it through the two unmistakable yellow goal posts.

Well on this day, we didn't live where ideally lived. The ball never reached the holder. We were doomed before we even had a chance. The ball never got off the ground and scooted right past Joe, straight to my feet. Without hesitation, I bent down and scooped it up, instinctively running to the right. We were coached to yell out "FIRE! ... FIRE!" when anything went wrong in the kicking operation to signal my teammates, who were facing the opposite direction that they needed to "HELP ME!" Well, I opened up my mouth and what came out was something like "EYE.... EYE", sounding like a pirate. I had never had to yell with a mouthpiece in my mouth before. Luckily for me, I wasn't the only one yelling and eventually my teammates got the picture.

As I ran to my right, all I saw was sky blue and maze, the colors of the day's opposition, Benjamin E. Mays High School. I was in prime position to "Get Lifted" in my John Legend voice. Between the defenders and the sideline, the world around me was getting smaller and smaller. Just before it was all over and as my eyes widened with fear, I saw a flash of white. Out of pure reaction, I let the pigskin fly. Somehow the first pass I had ever attempted in a game found its intended target, my teammate, Reggie aka "Earpad". It hit him square in the chest as he fell back into the end zone for the two-point conversion. The entire stadium roared in celebration and disbelief as if we had just won the game. I was shocked, amazed, and ecstatic at the same time. My second play in a varsity game seemingly destined for tragedy manifested into a phenomenal success.

As exciting as my moment was, we still found ourselves on the wrong side of the scoreboard that night losing 16-15. We started our season and my football career off, (0-1). Though the team lost, I came out of that game with immense confidence, thinking "This is gonna be easy!"

Now to the person who only reads for face value, that brief sequence of events was a highlight of some kid's high school hay day. Yeah, that was one of my greatest moments as a high school football player. But let's take a more critical look between the white lines.

We lined up with a plan with the intent to execute. In life we establish goals and plans to achieve said goals. It could be a goal you have achieved hundreds of times or maybe this is your first attempt. Either way your intent is to achieve it the way you envisioned. When something out of the ordinary occurs, like a bad snap, it creates an unexpected challenge. It requires us to react in the moment, while maintaining our focus on our preset goal of scoring. Through our preparation we performed in a pressurized situation and ultimately attained a greater success than the one we initially lined up for, two points instead of one. Our most challenging moments are often an opportunity to elevate and display the greatness within us.

Although we overcame one obstacle, which turned into one of the highlights of my high school career, we still were defeated in our ultimate goal.

Life hits like that sometimes. You make the plays you practiced and the ones you improvised, but somehow you still lose. You still get fired. You still fail a test or get hurt. This happens a lot. This happens more than you would think, but you always have a choice in what happens next. There is always something you can learn from defeat and failure. Opportunities come again and again as long as you show up, just like games on a schedule. Losing is going to happen, it's normal. Don't lose out on the experience of the opportunity. I grew quite a bit in that first loss. I gained the experience of playing in a varsity atmosphere and in front of a crowded stadium. I gained confidence in myself as a football player because this was the first game of my life. I gained the experience of witnessing the speed of the game, the physicality, the intensity, and some of the minor nuances.

We must challenge ourselves to see the growth in the good or the bad occurrences we come across in this life. There is something in losing that will prepare you to win. You must take your blinders off to expand your view to see it. When we are able to learn from these moments, we will be more ready to take on the next game, the next opportunity, the next season, and the next stage.

One play, a botched field goal that turned into 2 points, gave me the confidence to believe I could succeed in a game that was entirely new to me. The only way to even have a chance at tasting that delicious feeling of success is to step on the field and take a chance. Good or bad partake in the experiences to have something to learn and grow from.

CHAPTER 3 - PATHWAY TO PASSION

They say, "Your passion will lead you to your purpose." Football was undoubtedly my passion. I figured that out when I was four years old. This was the first time I saw Barry Sanders work his magic for the Detroit Lions. My heart was hooked on the game. However, I wasn't all in on my passion for a while. I took my talents to "South Beach." More like Southwest Atlanta baseball fields. I was pretty good at it, but baseball was just a tad bit too slow for a hyperactive child like myself. Besides that, it just wasn't football.

At five, I told my parents, "Baseball is too slow." My parents, learning who I was becoming, decided to move me into soccer. The goal was to run all that energy out of me. But neither of my parents nor I really understood what would come of this foreign sport. I took a bite into soccer, and it was sweet.

Soccer took my attention away from football just enough to buy my parents some time. One thing my parents taught at an early age was "if you're going to do it, do it all the way." Having that mentality, it seemed we would always find ourselves with the best coaches. Because oftentimes the best coaches look for the kids who work the hardest. I started to realize that if you showed people you wanted to do; they will go out of their way to help you. It may have been disguised as work ethic or just wanting to play. My desire in wanting to get better and wanting to be there, attracted the attention of coaches to spend extra time with me. It attracted them to want to push me to my limits to see how far I could go. It wasn't all fun and was often painful. If you do it all the way, you won't have any choice but to improve. At one point I was invited to play for the United States Olympic Development team as one of the better players in the country, but soccer wasn't my passion.

Though your passion drives you, your experiences mold you. There were lessons and skills in both baseball and soccer that I inherently adapted in preparation for who I would become. Even though it may not be what you want to do, go hard anyway. Do it all the way. We can't always be where we want to be when we want to be there. We can't always do what we want to do when we want to do it, but there are skills to develop in the places we do find ourselves that are guaranteed to elevate you when you reach the place you want to be. Who knows, they may be the vehicle that drives you up to the doorstep of your goals. Will you "do it all the way" to find out what the rabbit hole has in store for you?

THE DEAL

A year prior to my botched field goal turned success, I was in the stands watching passes thrown and touchdowns scored. Hoping and dreaming that I could be out there on the field under the Friday night lights. This longing had followed me around my entire life. My mother wouldn't let me play for fear that I might get hurt. But as a little man, my mother's sister, my Aunt Mae recognized how magnetized I was to the sport of football. She would walk me to her neighborhood park just so I could stand outside the fence and watch the other kids play. It was like she was taking me to the water's edge, the edge of my dreams, getting me accustomed to what it smelled like, what it sounded like, and what it looked like. It was going to be on me to feel it and taste it one day. Ten years after she had taken me to the fence for the first time I was at the water's edge, determined to dive in.

I grew up in a relatively comfortable setting, supplied with all the essentials of life and a few of the luxuries when things were going well. Even with everything I needed available to me, something wasn't right, and I knew it. In life, we will be innately drawn to certain things as if we are meant for them and they are meant for us. I couldn't explain why I loved it. How can you love something you've never done?

But I knew it was for me at an early age, and the feeling never wavered. We played in the streets, we played in the backyard, we played on basketball courts, and the tennis court. When mom and dad weren't around, I even played in the house. This was against the rules and punishable by thrashing. Occasionally I made an executive decision, and the whooping was always worth it.

One morning during my freshman year of high school, I was playing football on the tennis court before school when I felt a sharp pain in my ankle. I wasn't going to let a minor tweak stop me from playing, so I did the only thing that made sense to a desperate youth. I kept on hobbling around the court until the homeroom bell rang out. The pain continued and increased throughout the day until it became unbearable.

It turns out that that sharp pain was my ankle fracturing. I broke my ankle playing football on a tennis court. That's the story I had to tell people while I hopped around school on crutches for six weeks, but that's how bad it was burning inside of me. I was one of those "Wannabees" people talk about and laugh at, but eventually, I learned in order to be, you have to "want to be."

On the flip side, from this minor tragedy, I believe my parents got the picture. I was going to play football when and however I could, even if they weren't going to allow me to at least try the real thing. My mother realized how much I loved this game that she was holding me back from. I never let it down, always watching it, talking about it, and even acting it out as I walked around the house. She got the picture. "This boy is going to do it no matter what we say, might as well get some exceptional grades out of the deal."

Going into the spring semester of my 10th-grade year, she proposed a bet. The bet was that if I could maintain all A's and B's until spring ball started, I would get my shot to try the real thing. So, when my teachers thought I was highly interested in what they were talking about, I was actually chipping away at the wall between me and where I was meant to be.

Always a pretty decent student leading up to this point, I turned it up a notch. Whatever it was going to take to get the grades, I was down to do it. When that day came for those "foolish" teachers to supply those grades, they gave me exactly what I wanted. They gave me exactly what I had earned. My mother, being who she was, held to her word. I was finally given the green light to try out what my heart had always told me was for me.

In this moment, all I knew was I was going to get to play real football for the first time. Not only had I achieved my goal to play football, but I had also shown my teachers, my mother, and myself that I could do better than what I had previously considered my best in school. From that point on I was continuously held accountable from every direction to maintain that effort in the classroom because I showed it was in me. Through the inevitable conflicts and struggle with everyone holding me to a higher standard, nothing but good came from it.

Take note of what lies underneath the surface. When you are driven to do anything in life, you will be willing to develop, improve, and increase other unintended areas of who you are. Simply on your road to achieve. What are you prepared to overcome, to work through and learn, to get to that thing that's calling you?

CHAPTER 4 - PREPARATION IN DISGUISE

When I finally tried out for the football team, it was a culture shock. I had never run this hard. I had never been hit this hard, I had never been challenged like this mentally. When the final roster was unveiled, I miraculously made it, but not for the reasons I wanted. I tried out to be a receiver, believing I could follow in my father's footsteps. He played receiver and tight end in high school. I also wanted to channel my inner Jerry Rice, but I had a unique skill set that was rare for a black high school football team. Due to my soccer background, they immediately gifted me with the kicking duties.

"Aye kicker!" That's how I was addressed in my last two years of high school. Where I come from, the term kicker is defined as a non-athletic, soft, segregated, wimp. In my mind every time someone called me that, this was the disrespect I heard. A chip began to grow on my shoulder every time I heard "Aye kicker". I felt I had to prove how tough, how athletic, and how important I could be to the team.

Engulfed in an "I" and "ME" driven environment, the concept of "WE" was tough to comprehend. I wanted to be a receiver. I wanted to run routes. I wanted to catch the ball. "We" winning was not at the forefront of my preparation.

My ego just wanted to be the star like I like my favorite players on television. I was young and selfish. I allowed myself to grow a negative mindset, always seeing what I wasn't doing. I became determined to shed the stigma behind the nickname and redefine the term for myself.

In today's society, one of the hot topics is being transgender. The constant rhetoric that is expressed is that a transgender person feels that they are living a lie. Biology and society are telling them that they are one thing but, inside another being is fighting to get out of a hidden stifling place. A force deeper than the cellular level of their genetic makeup is in turmoil as they live a life that they know is not right for them. The electrical current rushing through your every voluntary and involuntary action is telling you "I know what I am. I know what I'm supposed to be." One of the greatest dilemmas for people who are in personal turmoil, is having an external force dictating who they are or what they are capable of doing.

Now I know that me wanting to play another position in football is not the same as being trapped in your own body clawing to get out and be who you feel. Not to minimize the plight of an oppressed people, but for me, it was! For me, it was just as powerful. The transgender plight is a societal example of what most of us go through at some point in their life. This is what I felt I was going through in my microscopic petri dish.

The frustration and torment were constantly eating at you, and feeling disrespected at every turn. The fight and determination to combat all the forces against you to be the person that *you* witness will take constant mental warfare. There will be a moment in your life when exterior limitations will be set upon you. You will have to decide for yourself to unleash yourself upon the world.

For the next two years, I was filled with frustration. It stemmed from who I felt I could be and who the world was telling me I was. The desire to be seen for who I knew I could be was great within me. I began challenging anyone at any time. I have been jammed up at the line of scrimmage countless times and even put on my ass a few times.

One day I called out the best corner on our team. He was also one of the best in the state, Addison Williams nicknamed "AD". He stepped up to my challenge with all the confidence he had earned. "Set Hut!" I made what I thought was my best move, but I didn't make it past the line of scrimmage. In fact, AD grabbed my shoulder pads, drove me out of bounds, and dropped me on the bench next to the water cooler. It was like he told me, "You look tired, little fella. Here, take a seat".

What most people probably would have done in this moment was sulk in embarrassment while the entire team laughed at the outcome. But when you feel it's for you, you will become a "sucka for pain." You will endure embarrassment, scrutiny, failure, and physically being beaten for the chance to be who you know you are.

I did what only made sense to me. I jumped up and ran back to the line, and called AD back up. He was the best, and I wanted to be the best. To be the best, you have to beat the best, even if it takes getting beaten over and over again. The next rep had a similar result. This time at least, I stayed on the field. I took an "L" and had to take the walk of shame to the back of the line to lick my wounds.

The next day I was right back at the line looking for AD. I lost a lot. On those few occasions when I would get a good release, run a good route, get open, or catch the ball … Well, those were the moments I began to live for. Those were the moments that made getting embarrassed worth it. A feeling of achievement would fill me up and fertilize my ever-growing love for the game of football and my ever-growing love of myself. The more I lined up, the more successes I would experience. Doing this allowed my confidence to swell. Success on the practice field began to become addictive even though they were few and far between. But I was still dwelling in the mental turmoil of not getting a chance to play on game days.

During my first season of football, when all I did was kick on game day, my father, realizing how frustrated I was getting, sat me down one evening. He looked me in my eyes. I felt him. I felt how grounded we were in the moment. That day he dropped some wisdom that helped me out of the ditch I was digging for myself. Of course, I stubbornly did not want to hear it. There was no way that he could understand what I was going through, but what he said to me was: "Riding the bench will be the hardest thing you have ever had to do, but just stay ready. All it takes is one play."

Eventually, I learned that the mental battle between my natural egotistical state and necessary humility would be harder than anything I had ever faced to this point. This was more than a battle. This was a war, a daily war. The power of our emotional mind is astounding. Unless you are made aware that there is a war to be had, it will control and govern your feelings, words, and actions without you even knowing. When things are not going the way you envisioned them, or you're placed in a position that you do not want to be in, how will you respond? Will you pout and feel sorry for yourself? Will you let your emotions cause you to act out and dig a deeper hole for yourself? Or will you recognize you are in a war? Will you fight forward not letting how you feel dictate how you act? Here's a secret: If you don't stand and fight for yourself, you will continue to find yourself controlled by circumstances rather than you taking the reins and taking control. I have been on both sides of that coin.

CHAPTER 5 - A GLIMPSE

Going into my senior season of high school, my team began to go to 7 on 7 passing tournaments around the state of Georgia. This turned out to be another opportunity to line up against some of the best in the state. I faced guys who went on to get drafted in the early rounds of the NFL Draft a few years later.

With our ridiculously talented number one receiver, Montrell Owens, stuck in summer school and unable to attend these camps, our quarterback, Cam, had to open his gaze and see the field instead of relying on his scapegoat, Owens. Opportunity surely waits for no man and appears on its own time. We must be a quintessential opportunist but understand opportunity is seized in the preparation, long before the moment is at hand. My first real opportunity to play receiver showed itself in the wake of someone else's misfortune. In Owens' absence, I was slotted in his place. I was full of anxiety, but when we stepped on the field, something happened. Unknowingly, failing against AD every day at practice prepared me more than I could have imagined.

It started with one catch, then another, and another. The catches soon became touchdowns. Touchdowns helped us win and from my success came RESPECT! It was a surreal feeling. I wasn't even a receiver on the depth chart at the beginning of the summer. Suddenly I became Cam's primary target. In the moment I didn't realize what was happening. I was engulfed in the opportunity. I was engulfed solely in the moment.

That summer my confidence grew not only on the field, but throughout all areas of my life. That reason alone is why we need to work into our passions. The effort of leaning into what you are willing to work for generates confidence in oneself. Confidence radiates from you and lifts your being not just your game.

The things I believed I could do and the things I worked on began to manifest. My negative attitude flipped 180 degrees. I became the most optimistic player on the team. I recall once in a tournament we were down with a minute left. I heard my offensive coordinator, Coach Daytona, say "Well, that's the ball game!" I stopped and looked at him and said "Coach we have time. We are going to get a pick and Cam is going to throw a touchdown to win the game." I don't know where the assuredness came from to talk to him like that, but when you feel like you earned "the juice", nothing is out of reach.

Two plays later the other team's quarterback threw the ball to the corner of the end zone. Instead of the intended target coming down with it, my nemesis AD picked it off showing why he was headed to the University of South Carolina. Our sideline erupted and I looked at Daytona. He couldn't help but smile.

We drove down the field in a couple plays, and with seconds left we had one opportunity left. "Set Hut!" I don't know the play call or the route, but Cam gave me a chance. He put the ball on a rope. I adjusted my body to intersect with the trajectory of the ball. With my eyes locked on I left the ground. With my arms stretched out to the max my hands latched on. It stuck as I came down and rolled in the end zone with no time left on the clock. I was trusted on the last play of the game to make a play for my team to win the game. My team erupted in celebration and stormed the field. They embraced me in jubilation, and I experienced a feeling like I had never felt before. The mauling love of my teammates filled me with pride. What was this feeling?

HUMBLE PIE

For some reason, I was overlooked when it came to tournament accolades. They would go to the same big names every tournament. It didn't bother me as much as it did my teammates. So immersed in the feeling every time I stepped on the field, I didn't care about the accolades. I was happy finally getting to do what I wanted to do since the first time I saw a football. The respect from my teammates was the icing and the cherry for me.

There are a lot of examples of people that received a lot in a short period and did not know what to do with it. This was one of those times. I began to smell myself a little more each time we stepped out there. I carried myself a little taller. I spoke a little more boldly. I took a sip of the Kool-Aid. The Kool-Aid, your aunt, used to make on a Saturday after that was sweet like syrup. Unaware of the happenings going on within me, this was my first taste of ego. It was oh so sweet, until it wasn't!

As life tends to do, I got more of something, just not more of what I wanted. Life can be a holistic comedian at times. The setup inflates your senses and hypnotizes you in a moment, then it drops the punch line on you, and you're the butt of the joke. Behind the joke is always a lesson to be learned to help us grow. I was given a strong taste of humility and the politics that are widespread throughout football.

At 16 years old, I didn't see any lessons, just the punch line. Going into the season, Montrell was back. I had earned my spot all summer, I thought. But, as soon as he stepped on the field, my role was suddenly decreased to that of a backup again. Montrell was an absolute monster on the field. I should have expected it, but what kind of competitor would I have been to concede a position I fought for daily in his absence. When you are in a position like I was, you have to do everything right. I take ownership of the fact that I gave the coaches the opportunity they were looking for to remove me from the rotation. I missed the last practice of the summer to go to the dentist. YES, "THE GOT DAMN DENTIST!" My teeth must have been that messed up to give up the opportunity I was fighting for, for the dentist.

Coach Daytona told me that because I missed this practice that I wasn't dedicated. All of the work, success, and all of the growth I had achieved in the summer was relegated back to just being the kicker. I was angry with the world and blinded by the hate that was filling the space that joy had resided just days before. Never get too high. It's a setup for a longer emotional fall. Never get too low because the mountain will begin to appear insurmountable. Stay somewhere in between so you can take everything in stride. You will be able to maintain the mental balance in this tight rope of life to keep moving in the best of times and the worst of times.

Have you had the bottom fall out? How would you have reacted in this situation? You think you're ready? Trust me, it's coming. Trust this also, with awareness even when you've been dropped on your face, you can push up, stand up, dust yourself off, and take the first step to get your momentum started again. I believe in you! Do you?

CHAPTER 6 - THE HARDEST THING TO DO

I was back to being who I was supposed to be, the kicker. Throughout my senior season, my frustrations continued to build. My dad, who was pretty in tune with who I was, noticed my demeanor. He consistently reminded me "It only takes one play, be ready." If you drown in how you feel right now, you will not be ready when it's your time!" As I reflected on what he said, I realized the truth. What I had done the previous season was exactly that.

"Be ready so you never have to get ready!" Coming to practice to get ready for my opportunity became my why. This was my last chance to play, next year was not an option. All I had was NOW! Everything we want won't always come in the time we want it, but with work it will come.

For the remainder of the season, he would have to repeat his message to reaffirm my stance and help me stay in the fight. He helped me remember why I should show up every day and why I should work hard every day in the shadows.

As we matriculated through the season, our leader, our quarterback, Cam continually showed that he was truly a man amongst boys. But somehow we started the season off with a 3-4 record. After an unbelievable loss to Northgate

High School, where I missed a kick at the end of regulation, that would have won us the game. The frustration of where we were, with all the talent we had, came to a head. The captains called a player only meeting to dig into the roots of our lackluster season.

As the meeting started it immediately felt like it was an all-out assault on "the kicker." Some of my teammates knew how frustrated I was, being the kicker. They knew that the kick I missed was a makeable kick for. They developed a theory that I had missed the kick on purpose because I was mad. Yes, I was mad. I was frustrated, and every synonym of the word. They began to tell me that I wasn't a team player, that I was being selfish, that all I needed to do was kick. The frustration I had been harboring began to boil.

First, my body began to heat up. Then I developed a slight shake. A drop of sweat rolled down the side of my forehead, and when I couldn't bear it anymore I rose to my feet. With everything that was festering inside me for the last two years I fired back. "You call me selfish, but I am the only person on this entire team who is forced to play a position that he does not want to play. I worked hard to earn a spot this summer. When all of our big names were gone I carried the receiving core." Now the anger and passion started to get the best of me, as I could not control it anymore. Tears began to roll from my eyes as I continued to stand my ground against what felt like the whole team coming at me. I could not fold because it was time to be heard, it was time to stand for what I believed. I believed I could compete with our starters who had been playing football since they were five and six. I believed I worked for a shot. I didn't ask for a handout, I wanted what I felt I had earned, and I was not going to take this mess from anyone who only saw me as what they labeled me as. In that moment, there were 60 guys looking back at me.

In all the fire that was building on both sides, something happened. The truth we were fighting to get to, shifted focus from the all-out assault on me to each position group, then to our starters, and other players whose effort was in question. We attacked every potential detriment to the team. The meeting turned from accusational to accountability. Accusations are divisive, accountability is empowering. Accountability is demanding ownership and responsibility from every part of the whole. This is what a true team does. No one is above the team. Even Cam got called out.

Though at face value this meeting was ugly, it was actually the counseling we needed to find ourselves in time to make a last ditch run to the playoffs. It was a moment for me to come clear to the world of who I was and who I wanted to be.

Looking back there was a flaw in my thought process. When you commit to being part of a team, you commit to doing what you can to help the team win. Even if it's not what you want to at the moment. Your time will come if you stay in the fight, but part of the process of life is being a helpful part of the community, the team, the organization, and the family.

We ended the season winning two out of our last three games, finishing up at an unimpressive, 5-5. But somehow, this year, that was enough to earn a playoff spot. It doesn't matter how you get in as long as you get in. But it does matter who are when you get in. A 5-5 record set us up to play the defending state champions of Statesboro High School. Statesboro is a city that lives for high school football. The entire city supportively stands behind their team. As we exited the bus we were met with a chaotic atmosphere. The fans met us off the bus and heckled us all the way to the side lines. They started down the roster spouting some pretty disrespectful insults, letting us know it was going to be a long night.

With all the excitement and intensity raging through the night, for me, it was rather uneventful. A lot of standing and watching, cheering, kicking, and standing again. Don't let my pity seeking demeanor cast a shadow on the story of that night. It was a dark, cold, biting night. Just the right environment for all the stars to align, and all of our stars were out to shine. The offense, led by Cam, was unstoppable. The defense was stifling, holding the defending state champs to 6 points. I don't think the state of Georgia had seen a team play like that the entire year. We dominated from the first whistle to the last. As I selfishly sulked in my little corner, everyone was partying and celebrating the biggest upset of the year. This could have been my last chance to play football, ever, and in my mind, I rode the pine all night long.

Even when the world around you is in a state of joy, thinking about the worst can leave you in a world of despair. Why do we choose to allow circumstances in our minds to govern our perception of reality?

LAST CHANCE

In the playoffs when you win you keep playing. Next up was Thomas County Central waiting for us to make a 4-hour drive to the Florida-Georgia line. We piled in busses and hit the road with the same focus that we took to Statesboro the week before.

It was a cold November night, when we finally made it to the town of Thomasville, Ga. As we entered the town it seemed there was no sign of life in the entire city. The streets were clear. The stores were empty. The only visible light was a glow in the distance. As we got closer, we began to see cars lining the streets. Next, we saw people walking in herds, all in the same direction. I realized that that glow I had seen in the distance was the stadium lights. We realized there was only one show in town, and it was featuring us. As we pulled up 2 hours before the game was supposed to start, the stadium was already halfway packed. The entire city must have been here to support their hometown team. I had never seen anything like it.

As I looked around the locker room, it was quiet. There was no hype, no dancing, and no singing. There was a focus and a power that everyone, including the coaches, was exuding. It was obvious we weren't shaken, we weren't rattled, and we were just as ready as we were the week before.

The game was a heavyweight fight, equipped with jabs, right hooks, body blows, uppercuts, and 9 counts. I can't remember how it happened or why it happened. In the midst of the biggest game of the season, and potentially the last game of the season the coaches looked at me and said, "Get in!" Vibes are infectious. In a moment where I probably should have been nervous, the confidence and calm my team had shown in pre-game nestled itself within me. Two long years of preparation allowed me to step onto the field with no hesitation. Trotting onto the field and into the huddle I looked Cam in his eye as he called the play. We lined down and got rolling, slowly moving the ball against the toughest defense we had seen all year.

On a pivotal drive in the 3rd quarter, we found ourselves behind the sticks. It was 3rd and 17. Cam gave me a dig route, 12 yards and in. This was the one route on the route tree I felt more confident in than any of the others. "Set Hut" Cam belted. I burst off the line, putting pressure on the DB covering me. When I got to my depth, I broke down and crossed his face. As I crossed his face, I turned to look back to Cam. He was under duress, but he saw me see him and he let it fly. Defender on my back, ball out in front, I left my feet, diving for the opportunity Cam had served up. My hands intersected with the path of the ball as I latched on just before I hit the ground. Because I had drifted up field when I came out of my break, the PA announcer came across the stadium speaker and yelled "First down Westlake".

That first catch always welcomes you to the game. You feel pulled into the synergy of what's going on out there. What made that catch feel even better was that we capped the drive off with a touchdown, allowing us to tie the game up.

Both teams continued to throw blows. With both sides of the stadium packed, the crowd was rocking. Darkness was engulfing everything around the school, but between the lights and the energy at the stadium we probably lit up on the map.

Third and Fourteen in the fourth quarter, down 21-14, Cam gave me the same route I had earned my first catch on. "Set Hut!" As Cam dropped back as I burst off the ball. Feeling the middle of the field opening up I put my foot in the ground and crossed my defenders face again. Standing taller than anyone else on the field, with pressure in his face, Cam was still able to see over everyone else and see me coming into the open space. Again, he let it fly. It was almost DeJa'Vu. With the defender draped on my back, I stretched out with every inch I possessed. The ball hit my hands and locked in place as the DB continued to swing wildly trying to knock it out. Again, the announcer rang out "First down Westlake" on the loudspeakers.

I stood up and tossed the ball to the referee. As I looked to the sidelines for the next play, I noticed a sea of white and blue erupting in excitement. Through two years of working, fighting, complaining, and believing, I was finally here in the moment. The moment I had dreamed of making plays for my team under the Friday night lights. The moment my dad told me I was preparing for. Through all the excitement and commotion, I found my dad standing on the top row cheering. It all came together in that moment.

We went on to score on this drive as well but, we lost the game, and just like that it was over. The dream pulled back into the station releasing the safety harness and letting all of us seniors off the ride. But not before I had one last run in with Coach Daytona, who never seemed to care for or believe in me too much. Somehow, we ended up face to face. Expecting some form of criticism, he stunned me when he said, "So that's what you have been telling us you could do!" That's all he said. He smirked, patted me on my shoulder pads, and walked off. I was frozen for a second. I didn't know how to respond. To me that moment meant I had earned a piece of his respect. I had never realized how important that was to me until I received it from him. Unknowingly he would indirectly push me forward in the not too distant future. "Coach Daytona, as much malice, as I held for you throughout the years, I take everything you helped mold in me with gratitude." What we go through, whether it be perceived good or bad, is part of the fertilizer of our lives.

CHAPTER 7 - I MUST LIKE HUMBLE PIE

Thinking this would be the last time I would ever strap on my helmet and lace up my football cleats had passed me, I turned back to soccer. I was hoping to get a college scholarship for those talents. With football over, I had two remaining goals to achieve in high school. Graduate and lead my high school soccer team to the playoffs. In the previous three years I was awarded team MVP, so to me, this was my team. To me, the success or failure of this team was on my shoulders. The "ME" and "I" mentality showed its ugly head again.

My school was not known for its soccer prowess. In fact, we were in dire need of players. At times we incorporated girls on the boy's team just to have enough people to play. With all of our deficiencies we still managed to make it to the playoffs my junior season. This was the first time in school history. Following that productive year, in which "I" scored 15 goals. "I" was poised to take the team back to the playoffs. However, as life had done before and as life tends to do, humility was right around the corner. We lost a lot of talent from the previous year, but "I" didn't think it would make much of a difference because "I" was still on the team. So "I" went into the season thinking "I got this."

On a cold night in early March, under the lights, we played the first game of the season against Creekside High School. At the end of regulation, the score was tied 1-1. This required us to go into a 15-minute overtime period and at the end of that no one had scored. On the rare occurrence that both teams make it to this point with the same score, penalty kicks are the tiebreaker.

Tied 2-2 in penalty kicks, it was my turn to step up to the penalty spot. A place that is as lonely as it gets in a team sport. You're one on one with the goalie. It's a place where the mind games begin on the long walk up from midfield. Staring down the goalie, you try fooling him into guessing the wrong direction while he is trying to intimidate you and stir-up any self-doubt that may be hiding within you.

In soccer, they teach you to have your spot. This is the place you go to every time. Don't worry about what the keeper is doing, perfect that shot. Perfect it to the point, that even if the goalie guesses right it won't matter. Your perfect placement will win every time. Imagine the goalie is not even there. All you have to do is put the ball in your spot.

My spot was the lower right-hand corner. I felt I could hit it with my eyes closed. I was beyond confident. I lined up, awaiting the referee's whistle. He blew it and I began my approach. Staring at the goalie, whom I thought was inadequate, I changed my mind mid-stride. "I'm going upper 90." In soccer terms, means tucking the ball in either of the upper corners of the 24' x 8' goal, which is a little more difficult. "Boom", I made contact with the ball. I watched it rise, and rise, and continue to rise. The ball went straight through the corner of the goal post, just not the one I was intending. It went through the lower 90 of the football goal post which hung two feet above the soccer goal I was aiming at.

My heart sank beneath my feet. My high horse had bucked me off. Creekside went on to score on their next shot and win the game. I had tragically let the team down and they humorously let me know about myself the rest of the season. This was a taste of what was headed our way all season. After that heart throbbing loss, another L hit the loss column. Followed by another and another. We then we were skunked 15-0. Followed by 4 more consecutive losses. We weren't even close. There is something to be learned, packaged, and taken with you in every occurrence in this life. You just have to learn to look for it. Sitting at 0-9 there was a mountain for us to learn.

As we went down this road of losing, the positive moments were few and far between. We began to cherish, appreciate, and thoroughly enjoy those moments. Those times we managed to put the ball in the back of the right goal became more meaningful. We celebrated each other. The look of excitement on my teammate's faces, who had never played soccer before, began to have more and more value to me. Understanding that supporting and celebrating all the members of the team cultivated an environment where the team could grow; an environment where we could grow was the real goal. Working like this allowed us to get better. We had even come close in a couple of games. We finished the season 0-10, but this was my first real lesson in leadership. You can find a golden nugget on your worst day or a golden goose egg in your worst season.

Could you show up and work as hard as you would during an undefeated season, during a winless season? Then can you show up and help your team attack the day for what it is, an opportunity. The awareness to search and dig below that topsoil is a skill that will be invaluable throughout your life. I challenge you to dig a bit deeper to find the diamond in the mine, or in your mind.

CHAPTER 8 - GRADUATION

Graduating high school is one of those monumental milestones in life. It's the personal accomplishment that is supposed to signify leaving childhood behind and stepping into your own-ness. The beginning of growing into the you that can stand on your own.

Graduation is a checkpoint, signifying a person has the heart and support to see a path to the end at that point in their life. After that day, the decisions are more heavily reliant on you. Each decision will incur the successes or consequences that follow.

It took me until graduation day to complete my senior project and get approved for graduation. I made it to and across that stage. After I took hold of my diploma, I felt it. The feeling of triumph and the feeling of completion. All the time, the experiences, the lessons, and work that it took to get here flooded my mind. My fist clenched tight around the rolled-up piece of paper that I later found out was a blank representation of the actual diploma. As I came to the edge of the stage, I found the section where my family had secured their seats. When I saw them, I stopped, and with all of the revered power I felt in that moment, I raised my clenched fist up as high as I could. I raised my fist in respect to these people whose hands prepared my food and whose shoulders I stood. The people that reached down when I had fallen to lift me back up again. My fist raised to the guardians I looked up and saw. They gave me hope that more was possible and that more was within me.

As I gazed up at them, all 20 representatives of my family had their eyes focused on me. As if choreographed, in unison they raised their fist in honor of how far we as a village had come. Family from all up and down the east coast were sending their energy to me in this moment. I felt the connection and the appreciation to have them there with me.

From those tantalizing first breaths of life, through me raising my high school diploma in triumph, these people guided my steps. They saw me before I knew who I was. They gave me the space to grow and the light to walk my path. Graduating is an important goal that soaks joy into the family community. I encourage everyone reading this book, if you haven't already done so, push through to finish high school. Graduate and clench your diploma. Tell the world and yourself, "I can grow, and I can achieve!" Stop right now and say it. Matter of fact go look in the mirror. Look in your eyes and say, "I can grow, and I can achieve".

You as a student, reaching this milestone in life is probably the first time you are truly confronted with the three tenses. You reflect on everything that got you to this point. All you learned, all you endured, all you overcame, and everything it took. This is your past. Your gaze begins to see a little deeper into why you feel, instead of just what you feel. The awareness of your past allows you to begin to develop a perception of who you are in this moment. The present. Crossing that stage is like coming to the end of a lit tunnel in the dead of night. The journey to this point has been illuminated by those who guide you. Go to school, go to class, come home, and graduate. You can't see the steps before you. You won't see them. You won't see the tragedy of hurricane Katrina ripping your life to shreds your first semester in college. Nor can you see the baby on its way that will change your life forever. You could never know the path to the scholarship you earned after walking on. You could never see the road that would take you to raising the Heisman trophy.

In the darkness that is the world every direction starts an entirely different path. Standing at this entrance or exit however you want to look at it, knowing who you are allows you to project an image of where you want to be. To reach the vision of your future, you must take steps into the darkness believing you are moving toward it.

Know that you will have more moments like this in your life and its ok if the newer you creates a new vision. Always believe your steps will take you to the ultimate you, even if it is in the complete opposite direction. Believe every step you take is a step toward all of your visions, especially the ones you haven't seen yet.

Then one day you will look back at the path you forged realizing the destinations you made your way to and through were only a small part. The journey, the obstacles, experiences, and beliefs earned along the way are what will mold you into who you see in the mirror. That will be the real greatness in you. Always remember "Life is a process, not an event!"

Graduation is the last championship of the first season of your life. Preparation for the next has already begun because there is no offseason in this thing called life.

The last note is to those of you who don't believe you will make it to graduation. The only reason you won't is because you believe you won't. Believe in you. Believe it's worth it. It's honestly not about the academics. It's about the lesson of pushing through a place you don't want to be. It's about pushing through a place you don't feel you're good at. It's about showing you what you are capable. You will hold on to that far longer than the empty diploma they will hand you as you walk across that stage. Push through!

SECOND QUARTER

CHAPTER 9 - WHAT NEXT?

Many of my high school football teammates had received full scholarships to go to school and feeling that I had been hindered from doing the same I became bitter. A scholarship did two things in my mind. It stated to the world you were good enough, but more importantly it was an opportunity to save my parents and eventually myself tens of thousands of dollars. It would help to prevent me from taking out massive loans and the interest that comes along with them.

That's what most people don't comprehend. A scholarship is not just getting to play football in college. Your education, room and board, dining, and books are all taken care of for free. Let's say the average college graduate leaves school owing $35,000. Check this breakdown, at a 5% interest rate when you leave school you will be required to pay a minimum of $375 a month to pay off your debt in 10 years. At that point, you would have spent a total of $45,000, about an extra $10,000 more than you took out. I think you could think of a lot of things to do with $45,000 at 32 years old.

I hope it's making more sense why it was so important to earn a scholarship. The work, effort, and success you have at 16 years old can have a lasting effect for the next 15 years of your life. Just because you are young don't think for one second that what you do today won't affect your tomorrow, and your tomorrow's tomorrow.

If you are in this stage of life or have younger loved ones, here is a well-known untapped source of debt reducing funds. There are hundreds of millions of scholarship dollars that go unclaimed every year from private sources. Most of which all you have to do is fill out the application and tell them why you deserve the money. There is another $2.9 billion dollars that goes unclaimed every year from government funds.

Yes, you have to go out and find these sources. Yes, you have to fill out the applications and submit the required documents. Think about it this way. If you spend 2 months doing this after you get home for an hour a day and you are able to nullify any potential debt. That's sixty hours to move $45k forward, plus the exponential value you build through your education in school. That's $750+ per hour of filling out applications. Does that seem worth it? I guarantee you can find a lot of things to do with that extra $45k in your pocket. Food for thought, to digest and implement. A good place to start is http://www.collegescholarships.org/financial-aid/

I'M TAKING MY TALENTS TO...

Before graduating I applied to the following 5 Universities: Howard University, University of Alabama Birmingham, Alabama A&M University, North Carolina A&T State University, and Georgia State. Because of the academic standards my parents and teachers required of me I was in position to get accepted to all of them. But, I had my sights set on UAB after watching Roddy White, Atlanta Falcons great, play there and get drafted. I believed I could go there and be the next him. After graduating and still not hearing anything from UAB about playing either soccer or football, I started to panic. Could this really be the end?

I started looking at the other schools that I had been accepted to hoping to squeeze my way into something. There was Howard, my mother's alma mater, Alabama A&M University, North Carolina A&T State University, and Georgia State. Georgia State did not have a football team at the time so that was out. I had a lead at Howard to play soccer, but they wanted me to pay my first year and it wasn't guaranteed that there would be money for me after that. Howard was about $4,000 more than my family had prepared to take on, so that was ruled out. It was down to Alabama A&M and North Carolina A&T. We decided to take trips to both of these universities with the intent of joining their football team and pursuing an Electrical Engineering

69

degree. Both schools had strong engineering programs and weak football teams.

This final decision didn't take long. If you ever make it to Huntsville, Alabama to the campus of Alabama A&M, and then teleport to Greensboro, NC and visit the campus of North Carolina A&T State University, you will never see Huntsville, AL again. You'll know why I put my whole focus on becoming a North Carolina Agricultural and Technical State University Aggie. After reaching this relatively easy decision, it was time to figure out how to get on the field.

On one of our visits to North Carolina A&T, my dad and I walked up to the football coaches' office hoping to run in to one of the coaches. We hoped to give them my highlight tape and convince them that I was worth giving a shot. We happened to catch the Defensive Line coach, Angelo Dixon sitting in his office. We introduced ourselves and I gave him my highlight tape which had film of me playing receiver as well as film of me kicking. Surprisingly, he stopped what he was doing and took the time to talk to us about the prospectus of the team. He watched all 3 minutes of my highlight tape, all 12 of my career receptions, and about 10 field goals. Four of those field goals were botched freestyle scores.

Watch how life works for you when you don't even realize it. I could tell he wasn't too interested in my receiver film, but neither was I. When the clips of me kicking showed up, I saw his whole demeanor change. He went from a controlled dutiful presence to an excited energy. "We need a kicker!" he exclaimed. I wasn't too enthused, but I ran with it telling him of my soccer background. We spoke for about 15 minutes and ended the impromptu meeting on a positive note. Coach Dixon was upfront and told us they didn't have any scholarships available and that he couldn't promise anything about walking on. He said he appreciated us stopping by and showing so much interest. As he walked us out, we passed a guy watching film who looked like a coach. Coach Dixon said: "Matter of fact, let me introduce you to Doug Brown." This guy who was in the middle of doing his own thing at the time jumped at the opportunity to sit and talk with us. We found out that Doug Brown is one of the most prolific receivers in A&T history and in 15 minutes he became my AGGIE hero.

We have to have heroes or people we look up to. They give us an example of the direction we want to go. These people reaffirm that our dreams are attainable. Doug was a four year starter at receiver. He held the record for most receiving yards in a game in school history. He was a fan favorite and was the ideal representation of what it was to be an AGGIE and what it meant to have "Aggie Pride." Doug removed any doubt I had about coming to North Carolina A&T State University. After that encounter, I forgot Roddy White. I wanted to be like Doug Brown. He became the symbol of who I wanted to become. After that meeting I knew there was a reason I had decided to take my talents to A&T.

CHAPTER 10 - THE SECRET

Graduation from high school was bittersweet. Sweet in a sense that I conquered high school. Sweet because my family, especially my mother, was abundantly proud of me. Bitter in that I watched 13 of my fellow football teammates walking across that stage knowing they were, headed to play college football. Schools like Florida, Kentucky, South Carolina, Western Michigan, Georgetown, Savannah State, and Tuskegee. I watched with a heart full of jealousy because I believed I was not going to have the opportunity to play the sport "I loved" ever again. Life works in mysterious ways!

Upon graduating, I was presented with an idea that would change my mind and my life forever. This idea was delivered in a very small package. It came in the form of a graduation gift from our neighbor, Joe.

In my neighborhood, the families were close enough to support each other in moments of celebration. As a child, my interactions with Mr. Joe were pretty limited. They mostly consisted of just saying hello. I would listen to Mr. Joe and my dad talk their old man talk on occasion. Though we didn't have a deep bond, he saw fit to present this young man, who he would see running the streets of the neighborhood with a life changing idea. Maybe he knew the effect that this $5 DVD would have on my developing mind. Perhaps he didn't. It's not always about the cost, but it is always about the value. Initially, I looked at the cover of this DVD completely uninterested because I had never heard anything like this in my small box of a world. My first thought was, this is some low budget indie film or something of that nature.

But...one evening when I was up to nothing. Something moved me to pop in the DVD simply titled *The Secret*. From this moment on, my life was forever changed. The DVD is a collection of testimonies and interpretations of this concept called the Law of Attraction. As it started, my skepticism continued to increase.

I had previously believed since I was a self-proclaimed good person that good things would come my way. I was respectful and always tried to do the right thing. However, this video taught me that wasn't enough. I had perceived hard times in my pursuit of football. Looking back at my situation I carried such a bad attitude, because I thought it was someone else holding me back from the potential, I felt I possessed within me. Between coaches, teammates, and friends, in my mind it was never on my shoulders. The blame was always pointing out and ownership was never taken within. I thought the kicker box

I was placed in was the width, height, and depth of my possibilities. The Secret taught me that the real problem lay within my thoughts which generated constant negativity. I carried this negativity with me every time I stepped out of bed.

The Law of Attraction is the magnetic connective power each of us has with the world we inhabit. Meaning the desires of your mind, good or bad will draw toward you.

"That's dumb!" were the exact words that came out my mouth the first time I heard this concept, but for some reason I kept watching it. As the documentary continued, the speakers began to express how the Law of Attraction presented itself in their lives. The information was starting to chip away at the walls of my closed mind. I began analyzing all the success stories I had ever heard. Those stories of Michael Jordan being cut in high school, but he believed he was greater than high school basketball. He believed and he worked as if he was just that, greater. Oprah Winfrey, who overcame a tumultuous childhood and an industry that did not want who she was, let alone what she could do. Her relentless belief brought her to and beyond the success only she saw. When Muhammad Ali said, "I'll show you how great I am!" It was a mindset; it was a belief!

Russell Simmons, Steve Jobs, and countless more have all claimed some parallel theory that got them to be where they wanted to be in life. They may not have used the exact terminology as this movie, but they all adamantly envisioned what they wanted in their life before any ounce of success manifested in their life.

I began to grasp the idea more and more. It told me that all the negativity I had bundled up inside me was causing me to generate negative thoughts which continued bringing unfavorable results in my path. Me and my unbelief that my coaches would play me, brought me and the bench into a long standing relationship.

For those who may think that everything in life is from God or your creator, you are not wrong. Try to look at it like this, God is the universe and God is in you! Most religions tell their worshipers to ask God(s) for exactly what you want in life, thru prayer. Be specific and consistent in your prayers as you worship that connective spirit. God will provide. The next step after envisioning, praying, and believing the things you want is going to work.

The Secret is not saying sit around and hope today is going to be a good day or that you will get that scholarship. It is not a passive act. The universe listens to you and conspires to put you and what you desire on a collision course. But, you have move to that point of collision. Believe it, see it, say it, feel it, and work toward it like it's yours. It may not always be in your time but stay diligent in your thoughts and work. It's coming! You have much more control over what happens in your life than you might think. Whether you whisper to yourself the good you want or you get on your knees at night and pray to your creator, the aim is the same. People just relate to different methodologies and that is perfectly ok. In my eyes, "The Law of Attraction" is the most rudimentary form of religion. Your connectivity to all that exists, because everything is interconnected, and everything matters. Your attitude matters, your perspective matters, your grind matters, your reactions matter, and your feelings matter toward the growth in your life. If we consciously take control of these things, then we take control of the potential of our lives.

Yea I know it can sound like some mystical, unrealistic, and over the top philosophical idea. However, if you really think about it, isn't the Bible, or the Quran, or any sacred book? It's about belief. These books are blueprints to that ultimate power we all live within. Really, whatever it takes for you to generate positive life altering beliefs, use that. I didn't connect with the Bible as a child, but *The Secret* was the ladle that began to stir my pot.

The next time something goes wrong in the morning, you stub your toe, or you miss your bus, take a breath. Catch your frustration, and simply say "I'm still going to have a damn good day." Dig in and find the energy to believe you will have a damn good day. Continue to say it throughout the day. Pay attention to how the day goes and how you feel about that day. Compare that day to the last time you let something affect your day. You will realize the difference is your mindset and your perspective. Being able to control the narrative of your own mind will open your eyes to opportunities that were once in your blind spots. You will be able to apply this "Secret" to all aspects of your life. If you don't like the way that sounds, stop, and pray your way through it. Either way, believe!

I watched this movie three times in a week. Each time it broke through another layer of my defense. I decided to try the principals that had been bestowed upon me. The first step I took was to do something my mother had been telling me to do since the day I was able to utter my first words. I got on my knees and prayed. In my youthful mind, all I knew was I wanted to play football again. I had yearned for the opportunity to play since I was four years old. I felt I hadn't really gotten a satisfying taste. Every morning when I woke and every night before I laid my head to sleep, I knelt beside my bed, clasped my hands, and prayed. I prayed out loud conveying what I wanted in my life. It went something like this:

"God, without question I know you support the brush strokes of the vision I have painted across my mind. Football, the emotional and physical outlet you introduced me to, is vanishing before my very eyes. A feeling in the deepest depths of my heart says I have more to give to the game and the game has more to give me. I pray to you with an open heart for another chance to show this world what you placed inside me. I know you do things with your vision and in your time. Please open an opportunity for me to play football in college. I will work harder than you have ever seen me work to be prepared when you reveal the door you want me to burst through. Thank you for all you have blessed me with and thank you in advance for the blessings coming my way."

No, it wasn't that eloquent, but I got a chance to write it, so I had to spruce it up. But it was along those lines. I prayed like this with the understanding that God was synonymous with the universe and that "The Law of attraction," was going to begin working for me in the direction I consciously dictated. I recommend that you get the book or watch the movie and just see what you feel. Let the greatest powers of the universe conspire on your behalf. Will you be ready when it's your time?

CHAPTER 11 - WELCOME TO COLLEGE

FOOTBALL

I went on for another two or three weeks in this way. I was going to an internship, training, being aware of my thoughts, and praying. During this time, my anxiety began to diminish. I began to develop the confidence that I was going to get a chance to play football again. When I was wasting time at work, I was on the computer looking at the A&T football roster. I was looking at the stats from the previous 5 seasons. All the way back to when Doug Brown had played. I envisioned lining up next to Curtis Walls, Chaz Dawson, Mike Caldwell, and Giorgio Lowrance who were the top 4 returning receivers.

I started running the mile that separated the train station from my job to make sure I got my conditioning in. I washed up in the sink before I went into the office. I was preparing for that call. I had the mindset that it was going to happen for me, and I was in it for the long haul.

One day my mother brought in the mail, and as she sifted through, she pulled one letter out and handed it to me. "I never get mail," I thought. The letter was engraved with the North Carolina A&T emblem glistening with gold. I began to open it with the thought that it was something about school registration, housing, or something pretty universal. However, what slid out of the envelope was the heaviest piece of paper I had ever come in contact with. On a scale, it would weigh in at the same 4.5 grams that every other 8"x11" piece of paper would weigh. But, the weight of the words on this piece of paper pushed me down into my chair. This piece of paper stated that the North Carolina A&T football team was inviting me to come to the 2007 North Carolina A&T State University football training camp. This piece of paper granted me preferred walk-on status. This piece of paper cracked the door. With the excitement building and bubbling within me, I looked at my parents and said "I'm going to camp. They invited me to camp!"

"It worked; the Secret worked!"

I would later find out that another guy had decided to go somewhere else at the last moment, so I was the fill in. The 91st man invited to camp out of 90, on the worst team in the nation. A&T was in possession of the longest losing streak in the country, but I couldn't have been happier. Perspective will be the difference in your attitude and mindset as you move along your path.

I was brought in as a preferred walk-on kicker. Yes, a kicker! The title I fought against for the last two years was now the life support to my aspirations. It's funny how life comes together sometimes. I encourage you to give all you can in every situation, even the ones you don't particularly like. You never know what seed you are planting to get where you want to be.

I was already in full training mode when the news hit, I didn't have to get ready because I stayed ready. At least I thought I did. As the summer progressed, I continued to use the techniques that I believed had given me this opportunity. When it was time to say goodbye to Atlanta, we hit the road into the unknown. I didn't know what was about to happen. The only thing I knew was that I'm about to make it happen. They don't know what they are about to get.

We arrived on campus August 2, 2007, the day after my 18th birthday. Fresh into a new year of my life and hatching into a new season. My parents dropped me off for registration where I signed in and made acquaintances with the managers and training staff who administered physicals. While sitting waiting for my turn to get evaluated, I hopped up on a seat next to this kid who was rather small. Small like, 5'7 130lbs., and had the same nervous facial expression I felt across my face. I don't remember how we got to talking but we did. Just so happened he was from Atlanta as well, from the east side. He had an extensive soccer background as well and he was brought to A&T on scholarship to be the kicker. We had too much in common for us to ignore. His name was Eric. As if it were destiny, from that encounter we have become lifelong friends ignited from that one interaction. It's funny how people find their way into your life, but it's incredible how people can stay for life.

My parents stuck around through the registration process and helped me move my clothes into Cooper Hall. This would be the dorm we would be staying in for the duration of camp. Cooper was an old school living residence. It had communal showers and dorm-style beds. The rooms came equipped with two desks and a closet. They were as basic as you can imagine. The one perk that came from being last was somehow I got my dorm room to myself.

When it was time to say goodbye to my family, to my support system, the embraces were strong and long. I had never been on my own for an extended period. Life went from 0-100 with a final wave as the car pulled away.

CONDITIONING

The next day it got real. After a 6 AM mandatory breakfast, we reported to the locker room to get ready. As I walked into Bryan Wellness and Fitness Center, the simple task of finding my locker became an actual task. Walking through every row of lockers, I began to think that they had forgotten to give me a locker. I went through every number until I reached the last locker with a helmet hanging in locker #106. I saw a piece of masking tape stuck to the top with "Miles" written in magic marker. A long way from the #5 I dreamt of wearing. They gave me a jersey with the digits 06 on it because they didn't have 100 numbers. Squared away with a jersey, cleats, and shorts donning "NC A&T FOOTBALL," it was time for the first true test of my college football career. The conditioning test.

At the start of every camp, there is a conditioning test to see if you are in good enough shape to begin camp. This year's test consisted of twelve 110-yard sprints. Each to be run under 15 seconds with approximately 36 seconds rest in between. It sounded easy enough, but what they didn't tell you was there was a way to run the conditioning test. Not knowing this particular secret, at the sound of the first whistle, I shot out like a cannon. I wanted to be noticed by the coaches but also by my new teammates. I definitely caught the eye of the other receivers like sophomore,

Giorgio aka "Gio" and junior, Chaz aka "Cheese", but not how I expected. After the third sprint, Gio, who was from the country parts of North Carolina, hit me with what I would learn was his catchphrase, "You better slow yo monkey ass down" I thought he was just mad that I was winning every sprint. However, I would learn very quickly that he was giving the most real advice I could have received in that moment.

By number 7 my legs had gotten heavy and started tingling. My lungs had begun to tighten. I could hear my heart beating in my head. Barely halfway through and my body was beginning to shut down. Each rep took everything I had to get across the line in time. The veterans had stayed the same pace throughout the entire test. They weren't racing each other; they were running their own individual races against the clock. Finishing one second early was the same as finishing 5 seconds early in this scenario. By the time we reached number ten, the battlefield was riddled with unprepared souls. Guys pulled hamstrings and caught cramps. Eric actually blacked out and the trainers were crouched over him trying to get him to wake up. As the whistle blew for number eleven, and everyone still in the fight took off I had this thought for the first time in my life. "Is this what you really want to do with your life?" with no real time to think about it, another voice responded, "Yeah bro, I'm down!"

Somehow, someway, and running like I had no knees, I finished my 12th sprint. I missed the required time on two out of the twelve. As I laid on the ground hoping the throbbing in my legs would subside. I knew I had failed the test, which meant I was going to have to endure extra conditioning during camp. I was okay with that. No matter how hard it got I knew I had made my decision. In the midst of reaffirming myself and my mission, as if a guardian angel were sent to welcome me to my own decision, Doug Brown ran over to me. He helped me to my feet and helped me learn to breathe again. After getting me upright, he jogged away saying "Welcome to College Football!"

Setting your goals is easy. You have a reason for them. They feel good at the starting line, but what are you going to do when you start the journey toward them when the journey isn't so easy? What do you do when the journey takes the oxygen from your lungs, the function out of your body, and the cohesiveness out of your mind? What are you going to do when it gets hard? Believe, my friend, and remember why you stepped foot on that path. Your body will heal. Your mind will settle, and you will be stronger for going through the pain.

CHAPTER 12 - CHANGE YOUR CLEATS

The next morning after recovering from the rude awakening that was the conditioning test, it was finally time to hit the field. Sitting in my locker at 7a.m., drowsy from being up so early, the locker room door burst open. It startled me. In walked a man that looked like he had lived a tough life and conquered it. He was the running backs coach, Coach George Ragsdale. His deep, harsh voice bellowed louder than I had ever heard a coach yell, "IT'S MOANAN' TIME!" Translation: "It is morning time" for all you scholars. I would later find out this outburst could have two meanings. One saying, it's time to wake up, while the other was an alert to let you know here comes the pain. Either way if you weren't awake, you were now. Ragsdale would make this a daily camp ritual. He was the perfect shot of adrenaline for those exhaustingly long days of camp.

Since this was my first time, I thought that meant hurry up and get outside. So, I rushed to get dressed. I grabbed my jersey, helmet, gloves, and cleats. The cleats were the key to the plan I had concocted. I brought two pair. One was a pair of soccer cleats that were much lighter and designed to have shorter spikes. Of course, those were to kick in. The others were true football cleats. The old school Nike Superbads, with long spikes to dig in and built for durability to survive the pounding football tends to inflict. If anyone was paying attention, it was a no brainer what I was about to do, but I went outside so early no one saw me.

There I was standing outside watching the sunrise. I stood fully dressed for practice with a second pair of cleats dangling from my hands. As players and coaches began to come out, I decided I didn't want anyone to see my extra set of tools. I thought of Joe Horn, the retired New Orleans Saints receiver. In a Monday night game, he hid a cell phone under the goal post pad and pulled it out after scoring a touchdown. So, I lifted up the padding on our goal post and stuffed my cleats underneath.

As practice began, we went through warm-ups. It was a routine of stretching and dynamic movements that we would repeat every day for the next five years. Next was a quick team learning period where the other kickers and I watched the team go through a few plays. Immediately following that session, the whistle screeched from right behind me as Head Coach Bob Mason yelled "Field Goal!"

There were three kickers, Eric, Elliott, a 6'5" lanky English kid, and I. Elliott supposedly had a legendary leg. As weird as it looked for Elliot to be at a historically black college, he never showed a lack of courage you would expect from someone thrown in the midst of a new culture.

We all jogged over to the middle of the field looking like some lost puppies looking for a treat. We didn't know where to actually go so we just stood about twenty yards back from everyone who was gathered on the field.

Eric went first and after getting off to a rocky start, he locked in. He showed accuracy and power to be so slight. Elliott was all power. He could kick a field goal from midfield, but if you were anywhere on the field you were in danger. His accuracy was erratic.

Up last it was my turn. As I lined up, I took my three steps back, two steps left, and added my patented foot twist signifying digging in. Making eye contact with the holder, I gave him a nod "SET HUT!" Just like high school. Unlike high school the snap and hold were more perfect than I had ever seen. As I started my approach, I saw that sweet spot of the ball rotating toward me. I saw it set up on the tee and I crushed it. I kicked the hell out of the ball. I looked up to see how far it went. Instead of kicking the ball sky high and through the uprights as I thought, the ball rocked straight ahead at eye level hitting one of our linebackers in the shoulder. A mixture of laughs and groans echoed across the field. I was pretty embarrassed.

Coach Mason's chuckling voice bellowed from behind me. "HIT IT AGAIN" "Hit it like a golf club, nice and easy stroke." So, I lined up again, dug in, "SET HUT" and sent the ball sailing down the middle of the uprights. "HIT IT AGAIN"! Bang! Bang! I hit two more in a row. The laughs around the field quickly turned into cheers of support. Then I did the worst thing I could possibly do, I started to feel myself. Humility will shine itself at that perfect mesh point of confidence and arrogance. I lined up three more times and missed all three of them. My inflatable head was deflated all the way to where the ants crawl.

As soon as I missed my last one, Mason blew his whistle again, "INDY"! Individuals was the period of practice where each position group separated and went with their position coach to work on position specific drills and techniques. As I looked around and everyone was going to their designated spots, I got a little anxious about what I was about to do. I looked at my fellow kickers. They looked like they were ready to go get a blanket and basket to set up a picnic on the sideline. I wasn't about that at all. It was at that moment I decided just to dive in. From the water's edge my aunt had taken me as a child, it was time to dive headfirst into my plan, my vision, and my dream. I ran over to the goal post. I took a knee, took my soccer cleats off and changed my cleats. I was unknowingly changing my stars and changing my life.

Standing up I took a deep inhale and spewed a calming exhale. I jogged, down the sideline, hoping not to be noticed by any of the coaches, to the receiver's line. I felt a few receivers stop and look at me but said nothing. When it was my turn the receivers Coach Mack Vincent, recognized I had infiltrated his crew. He paused and said, "Aye Boy!", in his Louisiana accent "What you doin?" Head still bowed, I replied, "I'm good coach" and took off into the drill. When I finished the drill, he actually threw me the ball. That action affirmed in my mind that I was a kicker no more. I was more than that. Going through that period, elevated my confidence. I looked around and thought "I can hang with these boys!" I did not participate in the rest of practice because I didn't know any of the plays, but my scheme was in motion, and I was "ALL IN."

There will be instances in your life that you will have the choice to take charge of your future, the future you see for yourself. Life can feel like you are being herded in the direction of everyone else. In doing so, you'll graze on trampled fields and someone else's waste. The moment you decide to pull away in your own direction you'll catch sight of greener pastures. Only thing is, you may have to go through the swamp to get there. Let your own passion lead your decisions and avoid the cattle syndrome society is built on.

Feel what pulls you. What illuminates your eyes when you see it and gives you butterflies when you're near it? Even if you're not good at it right now put your plan together. Work your plan. It may not be a split-second decision to dive in the midst, but all it takes is a split second to dive. Are you ready to change your cleats, change your life, and live YOUR life?

CHAPTER 13 - NEVER BACK DOWN

For the remainder of camp, I would kick and then trot on over sliding into the back of the receiver line for individuals. As I learned the playbook, I began to get a few reps here and there. First with the third team, where I made a few plays. It was enough to catch a couple eyes. Then a couple people got hurt and suddenly I was on the second team. "Be Ready!" Now that I was getting more reps, I had more opportunities to make plays. That was precisely what I did. My confidence grew with every success. So much so that the defense began to notice. Teammates and coaches wanted to know who this kid was that was giving them such a hard time.

"Are you a transfer?" "Are you on scholarship?" My answer was simply "No!" Seeing how confused they were when I informed them that I was a walk-on true freshman was always entertaining, but also inflating.

I already had a chip on my shoulder but adding a little helium to my head had me thinking I had arrived. Guess I hadn't learned that humble thing like I thought I did. Someone else went down with an injury. Three weeks after changing my cleats, I was running with the first team. These were the big boys. This was real college football. These were the guys who had experience playing on Saturdays and were primed to lead our team into the season.

Beginner's luck is a real thing. It's real because the novice person is mentally free. They don't know what not to do or what to be afraid of. Not having the fear of messing up or the fear of failing is powerful. Someone uninhibited by fear is dangerous and that person was me.

STAND YOUR GROUND

There is a saying that's out there that may not be the smartest set of instructions, but it's intended to earn you respect and let everyone know you're not a punk.

"Find the biggest, baddest dude on the block, and knock him out." Some of you may know how it really goes but we will keep this PG-13.

Something that stood out to a lot of my teammates was that I didn't back down. I didn't take any mess from anyone on the field. I was a little guy, standing at 5'10, 170lbs. The first opportunity I had to stand my ground might not have been my brightest moment.

We had an outside linebacker named Brandon Colbert, who went by only one name "Colbert". Colbert was literally built like a pit bull that walked around the back yard with the big chain around its neck and had the attitude of a junkyard dog to go with it. If you have ever seen Laron Landry who played at LSU and in the NFL in the mid 2000's, well they had to be his little brother.

I was under the impression he was on steroids, and everyone just accepted it. Later on, as I got to know him, I found out he never did steroids a day in his life. He just worked harder than anyone in the weight room. He paid more attention to what went into his body than anyone else. But I found this out later. At this point I believed he shot up for breakfast.

One day in practice I was having a pretty good day and I was letting everyone know about it. The defense was getting a little irritated with this freshman running his mouth. On one play, I caught an out route and was running down the sideline. As I looked inside, to see who was chasing me, who did I see? None other than "Colbert". I knew better than to try to bang him. I decided to cut back on him. As I made my move, he reached out with one hand grabbing my facemask and proceeded to lift me off the ground. He swung me around and threw me like a discus. My body went tumbling out of bounds. When I stopped rolling, I realized I didn't have my helmet on anymore. I looked up and saw he still had my helmet in his hand. My next move may not have been the best move, but it was the only course of action that fit. "I'm just going to have to die today" went through my head. I got up with no hesitation, no helmet, and squared up.

"What the hell is wrong with you bruh?"

"What are you trying to do?" was all he said.

I'm not even going to lie to you. When we made contact, I tried to push him with everything I had. For some reason I went backwards. That's not how a push is supposed to work. I began to realize he was 230 lbs. and obviously suffering from roid rage, but I couldn't turn back now. As we both cocked back to throw our heat seeking missiles, a wave of blue shirts came in and snatched me out the way of his rather large fist hurling toward my face. The entire defense came in and broke it up. Perhaps they didn't want this on their conscience. Whatever it was they swooped in and saved the day.

I may not have knocked out the biggest baddest dude, but after that encounter the word on the street was I had heart. From that one instance, sprouted the seed of respect from my new family. It's ok to get your beat if you stand your ground and fight for your place.

For those of you who were ready for me to get my ass whooped, that would happen down the line. However, everyone knew I was down for the get down. I continued that behavior throughout my first year. If the issue was on the field, it was handled on the field. Blocking drills often turned into rock'em sock'em robot fest. If you have nothing else to your name, you must hold on with your all you are to your respect. Fun fact, respect always starts from within.

BIG TANK

Another run-in that caught a lot of attention was with the biggest guy on the team. Tank Barker was the biggest and dirtiest offensive lineman I had ever played with. Tank flirted with 400 lbs. His idea of conditioning was sweating over the grill, which he was one of the best at. Envision that big stereotypical lineman from any football movie you've seen on the big screen. Louie Lastic, from Remember the Titans comes to mind, but grimy. Tank knew he was the biggest dude on the field, and he thought he could do whatever he wanted. His thing was to sneak up behind people and head-butt them in the back of the helmet. Often so hard that many of my teammates fell to the ground and one guy actually got a concussion. To him it was a big joke. As my teammates would be picking themselves up off the ground cussing him out, he would walk off belting his big deep laugh.

One day, after the final whistle of practice had blown, we started to walk to the locker room. Out of nowhere, "Bang"! I stumbled a few steps. My head was spinning. I had no idea what happened. When I finally regained my equilibrium, I saw him trotting away laughing. Realizing what happened, I didn't even think about it. I just took off running. He didn't see me. "You can dish it. Let's see if you can take it big boy." I said to myself. I took a wide angle and lined him up. I ran as fast as I could and closed my eyes. I hit him with all 170lbs. It felt like I hit a short bus. When I bounced off, I didn't think he felt me. When my eyes opened, I was shocked to see all 400 pounds of Tank crashing onto the ground. I paused in shock, but satisfied in the same moment.

He let out a loud yell as a little fear added itself to the mix. I thought he was hurt. Four hundred pounds doesn't fall gracefully. He had to be hurt. I had just seriously injured our starting right guard." Another thought crept in my mind. "His big ass is going to get up and try to kill me. Those thoughts went away when I realized his loud yell had turned into hysterical laughter. He knew what happened before he even saw who it was. For the next 15 seconds, he lay on the ground just laughing. Our head coach came over to check on him and he just kept laughing. When he was finally helped up, I was still standing there frozen. Still laughing hysterically, he looked at me. I asked him if he was alright. Able to stifle his laughter for a few breaths, he responded "Yea, I'm good little fella." He told me I had just earned his respect for life. He said in all his time at A&T no one had ever retaliated. Not even his fellow lineman. He also told me that from that moment on he would always have my back, which he did from then on. He always reminded me of that day. He would tell people that "Little man got heart!"

For a person who respects themselves and is working for a goal, earning your respect is crucial. Our intolerance of disrespect is key to our personal development. Your self-respect and self-love should not accept disrespect from the outside world or from within. You know your true worth and the potential within you. Allowing others to hold you back, tear you down, or step on you is unacceptable. The more you fight for your respect, the more the world around you will begin to hear and understand you are here to stay. It can be a long road, but it is necessary. Stand up for who you believe you are. As much as your family and friends want to do it for you, there will be a day when you're in a corner and the only person there to fend for you is you. Be it in the classroom, in an office, in your home, or on the field. The one that will have to stand their ground is "YOU!"

Understand there are different forms of gaining your respect in the public eye, but you must start with your self-respect. You don't have to punch your classmate in the face to gain your respect. People really just want to see if you will stand up for yourself. It took more than a couple fights to establish my respect, but they are part of a series of events to put everyone on notice. Eventually I did get across to the entire program that I would stand for my respect every ounce of it. Are you prepared to fight for IT? What does your fight look like? Wars have been won without a single blow. Go out every day and compete for your respect. Fight for the person you are and put your heart out on your field. "Never back down from yours!". They will respect you when you respect you!

CHAPTER 14 - MOTIVATION LIVES EVERYWHERE

As camp continued on, I continued to excel. My confidence was soaring. I was on pace to come in as a walk-on kicker and start the first game as a receiver in my freshman season. Watch *The Secret* work. Before the season started, I was presented with a real jersey, with a real number. It was the jersey I envisioned all summer. It was the number 5, just like Doug Brown.

A year previous I was losing day in and day out to AD. Those losses were preparing me for the victories of today. No one I lined up against at A&T compared to battling against AD. Our failures are opportunities to prepare us for the success of our future. We must keep pushing even if we aren't winning today.

I was preparing my body all summer long for this opportunity. It seems I may not have been training the most important part of the body. With a week left in camp and the start of the semester, the guys that were hurt were starting to come back from injury. Although I was still playing well at practice, I began to feel the pressure. It started with a few missed assignments. I started lining up wrong or running the wrong route. I even dropped a few passes.

My focus was all over the place. Living on my own for the first time and being responsible for myself was different. I lost my focus to the distractions campus supplied. I was learning where to go, making time to eat, going to weight training, classes, study hall, girls, meetings, and practice. This was a new test of my organization and discipline, and I was failing.

Toward the middle of my first week of school, I was informed that I was being demoted to the second team. They had no plan to play me even though I would dress for the games. This was really more than I thought would have been possible coming in as a walk-on kicker. I missed out on an opportunity because I wasn't mentally strong.

Along with this news came the weight of my daily schedule. Something they don't portray very well in sports movies is the true grind of the collegiate student-athlete. This was my schedule my first semester of school:

5:30 AM	Wake-Up	12:00 PM	Class
6:00 AM	Weight Training	1:00 PM	Lunch
7:00 AM	Breakfast	2:30 PM	Meetings
8:00 AM	Class	4-6:30 PM	Practice
9:00 AM	Class	7:00 PM	Dinner
10:00 AM	Class	8:00 PM	Study Hall
11:00 AM	Class	9:00 AM	Study Some More

Two weeks before the start of school I thought I was on my way to stardom as a starting freshman receiver. Now I was getting red-shirted and getting crushed by the life I thought I wanted. Going from being at the bottom to rising to the top, to scavenging on the bottom once again can happen in a few instances. Humility will find you and will bring with it reality. This frustrated me, but more importantly it motivated me to always work to be mentally and physically ready.

RAGS TO DREAMS

North Carolina A&T was coming off a 0-10 season. The morale and heart of the team wasn't great. A&T had been hit with a few sanctions by the NCAA because the graduation rate was ridiculously low. Guys would come in, play two years, get in trouble, or have very poor academics, and leave. They pretty much did everything except finish through and graduate. A&T's football scholarship count was cut in half as a result of what was happening off the field. We went from 66 scholarship athletes. On top of that all out of state student-athletes on full scholarship counted as two full scholarships. This was as close to the death penalty as a D-1AA program could get without dying and our record showed it.

Understanding where we were mentally as a team, Coach Mason tried to create some enthusiasm. He set the stage for one of those transcending moments you don't expect, but you know when you're in it. He introduced Coach Rags, the "MOOAAANAN TIME" guy, to speak to the team during a meeting. Rags played at A&T in the 70's. He is an A&T Hall of Fame running back, who had gone on to the NFL where he was drafted and played for the Tampa Bay

Buccaneers. Rags had a different respect from the team, partly because of his connection to the program, but mainly because he represented the dream, and how he connected with the players themselves. At 55 years old he smoked cigarettes every day but would get out there and run sprints during conditioning with the team. Unfortunately, he beat quite a few guys.

Rags approached the front of the meeting room, and as he reached center stage he bellowed in his deep raspy voice "Well listen, fellas..." He talked about the uphill struggle we found ourselves in. He explained that we would have to ignore the distractions, focus on the guys in the room and that at some point we as men would have to take responsibility for the future of the program as well as our own futures. The room was silent. All eyes and ears were locked in. Rags paused and scanned the room. Then he plugged something in my brain that would nest itself deep inside to germinate.

He said "I want all of you to do this. Take a look to your left. Now take a look to your right. Look all around this room. Of the 90 guys in this room, only one of you is going to get a shot in the NFL!"

In this moment more than any other, I felt he was talking to me. I had never had dreams of making it to the

NFL before this moment. I felt fortunate just to be in the room. But, sitting in the back row where the light was dim, a light went off in my head. I looked around the room and, in my head, I apologized to everyone. If it was going to be only one guy in this room that made it to the NFL, I decided in that moment it was going to be the walk-on kicker from Atlanta, Ga. I had never felt this was even possible before this moment. I don't know how my teammates received this message from coach Rags, but I took it as a bond to work as hard as possible to achieve.

SEAN TATE STRIKES AGAIN

Remember the offensive coordinator that I felt doubted me so much in high school? Well, his name was Sean Tate. I heard a rumor he attended A&T at some point. The last time I saw or heard from him was that night that was supposed to be the end of my football playing career. He doubted me so deeply. He was a source of anger and drive whenever I thought of him. I had allowed him to have control in my mind. The funny thing about being mad at someone else is most of the time they are completely unaffected. The only person hurting is you. It takes a conscious effort to prevent others from affecting your thoughts, your mood, or your progress. It's yours for a reason. Tate probably never thought anything about me ever again and here I was 300 miles away combating the hatred I had for him.

Well, I thought I was 300 miles away. One day while I was in the coaches' office waiting for a meeting to start, I began looking at all the team photos of the past. Teams from the 70's, '80s, '90s, and early 2000's. As I gazed into the past, I came across an all too familiar face. It was Sean Tate, sitting cross-legged front and center, smiling from ear to ear. I was shocked to see him sitting there looking back at me. I didn't have the reaction I would have imagined when I saw him. A grin began to form, and it continued until my smile matched his, ear to ear. Seeing him didn't inspire hatred anymore. It excited me. I remembered that I used to work so hard for his approval. No matter what I did it never seemed to be enough.

I laughed because I was going to be able to walk past this picture every day and I knew it was going to motivate me. The motivation was no longer to get his approval. He was the symbol of everyone who thought I was just a kicker and had no further potential. Seeing him everyday front and center cheesing was the reminder that I knew I had more than any of them could have imagined within me. Seeing him reminded me every day to show the world what I believed.

Motivation looks different for all of us. It can come at the most random or opportune moments. When you see it, when you feel it, embrace it. Use it to push harder and to do so consistently. Use it to remember why you are doing whatever your it is.

What parts of your life currently motivate you? What is it that triggers an abundance of energy within you? Is it your current living conditions? Is it watching your family struggle? Is it the want of nice things? Is it to confidently look in the mirror? Whatever it is, feed off the energy it produces.

CHAPTER 15 - KICKOFF

As the season began, I was redshirted. A tough pill to swallow after how much success I had during camp, but I had been here before. I was prepared to give it all to my team in practice knowing I would not see the field on game day. Pops said it would be the hardest thing I would have to do. He was right, in that time. Since I had the experience of sitting and waiting, I was ready for this. I knew what I had to do, and no one could understand why I practiced so hard and had so much fun not playing.

Warm-ups for the first game were intense and focused. Both bands were rocking the ground beneath us. The stadium was filling up with more people than I had ever seen come to watch my team play. As the stands filled, the atmosphere began to rumble like the drummer boy building the rhythm for war. Being on the sidelines listening to the conversations, the strategies, the conflict, and resolutions was intoxicating. Our team came out with a crazy energy. The desire to hit someone else was evident as the countdown to kickoff began. Even Eric, who had won the kicking job, was juiced up.

Across the field stood one of our rivals, Winston Salem State University. They matched our energy blow for blow and were the better team by far. By mid-way through the second quarter, all of our excitement was gone. They smacked us in the mouth over and over again. They ran all over us and it got very ugly very quickly, ending in a 28-7 thrashing on opening day.

The worst part about red shirting is you are helpless to help your brothers in a fight. The best part of redshirting is you are able to watch up close the do's and don'ts in preparation for your day.

HEAD ON A SWIVEL

I did a lot of learning that first year, on and off the field. So much to see and experience. So many people to meet and so much schoolwork to do. To grasp it all you had to be truly aware of your surroundings. If you weren't it could end in tragedy. One instance drove home that point for me that year, more than any other.

Eric and I walked to 6 AM workouts every day. We had gotten accustomed to seeing one of our teammates driving by who would stop and give us a ride. One morning was a little different than all the others. It started out with us getting caught by our building's security guard going out the emergency exit. This was supposed to be prohibited before 7AM. We had been eluding him for weeks, but he got the drop on us this day. We took off running through the building in the opposite direction to elude capture. After our run-in with our nemesis at 5:30am in the morning, with our adrenaline still pumping, we headed down the street toward the weight room. Like clockwork a car rolls past us and pulls in the middle of the street and stops. On queue Eric and I, still excited from our startling encounter, ran over to it. I pulled open the front passenger door and hopped in. Eric jumped in the back. The car doors were unlocked, so there was nothing out of the ordinary until out of nowhere, I heard "Oh Shit!"

It was strange, but neither Eric nor I comprehended what was really happening. I turned and said "Preciate it bro," but as I'm looking at this dude, I didn't recognize his face. He never even looked at me. The guy starts driving so again I'm thinking everything is cool. Then he makes a left down the middle of campus, which is not the way you would get to the stadium. Still trying to figure out who this dude is, we continue to ride. If I had been any kind of sleep, I was all the way awake now. I looked at Eric in the rearview mirror and he was staring just as hard as I was at the dude. We slowly creep into a parking lot and everything starts making sense. I didn't recognize him because this guy didn't play football. We were parked in front of the ROTC building. ROTC had 6AM workouts as well. We had jumped into a random dude's car at 5:45 in the morning. "Oh shit" was right.

He had to have thought he was getting robbed. We scared the life out of this guy, but I have to give him credit. He handled it better than anyone I could have imagined. When we finally stopped, I assumed Eric came to the same conclusion. The second the car stopped moving, I heard the back-door pop open, and he took off running. He left me there apologizing "I thought you were on the team bro!" The guy still never said a word, nor did he look my way. I hopped out the car, politely closed the door, and took off after Eric sprinting through campus. When I caught up to him, we were both laughing hysterically. We made it to the gym at 5:59AM just in time to prevent Coach Prince from having us doing something crazy like rolling on the wet grass in the dark.

We laughed about it, but that situation could have gone entirely different. I know a lot of people who carry a weapon with them in the car. Since we were unaware of our surroundings, things could have gone wrong very quickly. We must always pay attention to the details. The details will literally save your life.

"Keep your head on a swivel." This is a phrase we use in football that means be aware of your surroundings, because if you don't it could be lights out. In football there are dangers and opportunities all over the field. We have to constantly scan the field to see and feel where the hit is coming from. We have to see where the opening is. We have to be aware of our surroundings, so we don't get blind-sided. Be it a business move, career move, relationship move, life move, or juke move to avoid Ray Lewis running through you, "Keep your head on a swivel" and you will give yourself a chance to respond accordingly.

In the video game Madden, each player has a list of attributes like speed, toughness or catching. Each attribute carries a rating from 0-99. All of the best players have high awareness, because of how vital it is to see and understand your surroundings. Awareness is the difference between good and great. It can be the difference between life and death. Improve your awareness and you will improve your life. What is your Madden Awareness rating?

CHAPTER 16 - INSTANT CLASSIC

If you ever find yourself in Greensboro, North Carolina, take exit 39 on Business I-85 to US 29 Reidsville. When you see the sign for East Market Street, take that exit and transcend into North Carolina A&T State University. One of the first things you will see is a towering smokestack that reads AGGIELAND, spelt vertically as if reaching toward the heavens. At A&T there is this thing called "Aggie Pride". It's the connective spirit that binds all who take the journey through the esteemed halls of A&T's campus.

I got my first true introduction to AGGIE PRIDE the night we played our biggest rival, the eagles of North Carolina Central University. The blood between these two universities is beyond bad. I think they hated us because we thought we were better than them. Side note: "We are". Whatever the real reason was, it was long buried underneath decades of hatred.

To this point we had not won a game, but the rivalry ignited a fire within us to do whatever it took to beat these buzzards. Practice was different, meetings were different, and campus was different that week. The hype and the buildup were compelling. The game itself didn't disappoint. It turned out to be an instant classic.

They couldn't stop our running back Michael Ferguson. He seemingly broke a big run on every drive. We couldn't stop their screen game. They scored two long touchdowns, running the same screen to the same guy. The game came down to the last drive. In the calm night, both sides of the stadium were blasting. I was allowed to dress this week again. On the sideline, looking up at the chaos that was whirling around us, I was in awe. We drove down the field to the 6-yard line. It was like someone plugged in the subwoofer because the bass of the crowd noise intensified. Fourth down with seconds left on the clock and we were down by five.

We called a pass play because we knew they were keying in on Mike. Our quarterback, Damon Stewart, took the snap, dropped back faking the handoff to Mike to draw the defense in. It didn't fool their outside linebacker. He dropped into coverage. Rolling out, Damon, made eye contact with his target. He tried to loft the ball over the linebacker and into our receiver's hands. The ball wasn't in the air for a whole second, but like a scene from a movie, it seemed to be in slow motion forever.

My teammates and I were on the sideline holding hands and praying, as was every member of the crowd on both sides. As the ball sailed through the air to its open target, suddenly a soaring eagle with a white jersey and burgundy helmet flew by snatching it away. One side of the stadium erupted in celebration, while our hearts dropped onto the ground.

They celebrated loud and proud, adding another loss to our record. This one was a dagger because of who was on the other sideline. They celebrated on the field like any other team would in that situation, but what really made this night even more of a blockbuster was kicked off by what they did next. Their celebration quickly moved to the center of the field where the Aggie bulldog was painted. They began stomping on it and pointing at all of us, coaches included. When disrespect is in play it's almost instinctual to confront it.

Somehow, I found myself on the front line of our team walking out to meet these disrespectful buzzards. Imagine two armies squared off chomping at the bit to attack waiting for the spark to light the powder keg. Well, that spark came in the form of our quarterback bursting through and diving into them taking one of the buzzards to the ground. When one goes, we all go. That's exactly what happened. BLUE and GOLD collided with white and maroon. I collided with a white jersey and started swinging, but my fight didn't last too long. That night the cops were on their job. They began spraying pepper spray into the brawl. I don't know where it came from but, somehow, I got a full stream square in the face.

If you have ever been hit with Sabre Red – tactical pepper spray, you know it feels like your eyes are boiling. It chokes and burns your nose and throat. In an instant I was blind and unable to breath. Not the best obstacles to be battling while in a fight. I stumbled back a few steps, one hand wiping the pepper spray deeper into my eyes and one hand swinging wildly. Standing back watching me, was probably pure comedy.

As I kept backing up, I felt someone grab the back of my shoulder pads. Before I could wheel around and engage them, I heard a voice say, "Relax." Trusting this voice, I stopped swinging. He guided me to the sideline, still choking and gasping for air as I continued rubbing the fire into my eyes. He grabbed a water bottle and began dousing me with water. After he got me situated, he walked away. I never knew who that calming savior was that guided me out of the brawl. Thank you, whoever you are.

At times we all need an angel to swoop in and grab us up to save us from the chaos we put ourselves in the middle of. It may come in the form of a coach recognizing some troubled behaviors and taking some extra time to teach you by helping you with your classes. A mentor reaching into your life and pulling you out of that car that is headed toward a robbery. It may come as a godly whisper in your ear, guiding you out of your self-destructive behaviors. Feel, hear, and realize when an angel appears in your life to help move you out of the madness you are headed toward. It's ok to listen.

Did you expect that story to end like that?

CHAPTER 17 - THE OTHER SIDE

As student athletes we often don't pay as much attention to the student part of that combination. Education was forced on me at a young age, so I was inclined to try to do well in school. In those times when I wasn't in the weight room, the cafe, in class, or practice I was putting in extra time studying. It paid off. I finished my first year with a 3.0 GPA, not perfect but I was proud of it because I knew the work I had to put in. There were many nights I had to miss the party. I had to miss events. I even had to miss the girls. Sacrifice tends to lead to positive progress toward your goals.

When we are growing toward the vision of who we want to be, understand that we can have everything we want in life. But also understand that you can't have it all at one time. If we want to be well rounded in our goals, we have to break our development up into seasons. A season is a time period for anything in your life. Just as the year has seasons so does life. Just as the seasons bring different attributes to the Earth's climate, the seasons in our lives bring different climates for us to grow through. These different seasons require us to grow and develop different attributes of the whole you. We have to intentionally decide what those attributes are, and focus our intent to grow those disciplines.

Focus on learning the plays, playing hard, and catching the ball with your hands. Don't worry about how you ran the route, what the defense is doing, or your swag on the field. Why do you think you only have a certain number of classes per semester in school? You spend five months learning a few disciplines that lay the foundation for the next semester, the next season. Understand this philosophy in your education and into your life's aspirations. But we have to harvest all we can from each season, because your future seasons are bound to require some of the foundation from your current one. If we don't take advantage of growing right now, we will begin to get left behind. That already tremendous mountain will begin to get taller and longer.

Once you have gained a mastery of your initial set of concepts, then you are ready to adjust your focus by committing to the next set of concepts while retaining everything you learned before. We go through the same process of being intentional in our personal development. Mastering a few tools at a time will load your tool bag and you will be ready to go to work in any situation you are thrown into. Though the human mind is truly one of the wonders of the universe, we can still only focus on maybe three things at a time effectively. When we try to overload and learn everything at one time, we aren't able to latch on to the details that are truly the difference in managing and mastering.

EXIT INTERVIEW

When the year is over, every player must go through an exit interview with their position coach. There I was sitting one on one with Coach Vincent. At this time, we didn't really have the best relationship. This was partly because I felt he talked down to me. It was mostly because I had a smart mouth, and he wasn't going to take any of it. We both felt there was a lack of respect in play so the tension in the room was thick.

Side note I called him Marcus one time to his face and in mid-sentence he squared up ready to box it out, saying "Boy, I ain't ya friend. You betta put some respeck on my name!" years before Baby showed up to The Breakfast Club. It must be a Louisiana thing, but I digress.

In this meeting the coach is supposed to give you feedback about the past year and what the staff is expecting from you. I've learned to take the positive for what it was and to do the same with the negative. But as a freshman I took it all personal. He started the conversation talking about how I didn't listen and then went on about my abilities. This is where I sat up to pay attention and listen, because although we had our issues, I respected Coach Vincent's knowledge of the position. I respected his opinion when it came to the field.

He started off saying "You're slow!" followed by "You catch like 7 out of 10 balls. That's not good." I tried to reply, but he kept going. "You're weak!" "Your routes need a lot of work." At this point I'm glaring, but I decided this was not the time for us to argue. This was a time for me to hear. With everything boiling within me, I managed to keep quiet as he continued to pick me apart. He never said it but what I heard from that meeting was "Boy, you suck!" in that Mack Vincent voice and for some reason it cut deep.

Years later I realized, and he admitted that he rode me so hard because he saw something in me and didn't want me to be complacent in the small success I was having. I felt that he had a vendetta against me, but what he actually had was my best interest at heart, it just didn't look or feel like it. What we see and feel is normally from one perspective, our own. We only see what we see, and miss the other angles. We allow our ego to narrow our view. Coach Vincent's goal seemed to be to break me, but his real goal was to make me.

But in the moment, I had no idea what his motives were. I could have gone in the tank after my meeting. I could have said "Forget you, Marcus", or accepted football just wasn't for me. I was enraged walking out of the meeting, but unknowingly that meeting was empowering. Sometimes we need to hear our deficiencies, plain and straight. If we always hear how great we are it is easy to develop a sense of complacency. I walked out of that meeting with an, "I'm going to show you" kind of anger. In my seasons with Sean Tate, I learned to respond to words, with action. With that, my first year at North Carolina A&T was over.

How do you receive criticism? We are allowed to feel however we feel. Let the energy build within you, but don't let them see it. Don't allow that energy to implode. We must take that energy and funnel it into the fuel tank of the vehicle driving toward who we see ourselves to be. The greatest response to criticism will always be taking it for what it is and then propelling yourself above the critique.

CHAPTER 18 - OUT OF THE BOX

After the school year, I headed back to Atlanta. I was set up to return to an internship I had the previous summer with Jones Consulting Engineers. This year I planned to go back up to school early to work out with the team. I was only going to get about 6 weeks, but I wanted to try to earn as much money as possible in that short period. Years later I would realize that being there was not about the money, but more so about the knowledge I could gain from the work. The conversations with my coworkers were extremely beneficial. Experience is more valuable than any dollar. It's what will put you in position to make the dollars you want later.

I was working on what was perceived to be my future career. I would be sitting in front of a computer, drawing up plans and doing math. This was great but, I was really focused on what my heart was yearning for. I continued my morning runs from the train to the office. On days I drove, I would go to Doctor Lacey's Intensity Healthcare training facility after work.

Jones Consulting Engineers was a good experience for my life. It felt like, the owner, William Jones took an interest in me and treated me as if I were like every one of his salaried employees. He took me to work sites so I could get a visual of how parts of the design translated into the real world. It was a little odd for me. He was this older, southern, white man who seemed comfortable enough to bring this young African American teenager into the business that he worked to build for decades. Where I grew up, we assumed someone of his stature would judge me the moment the name on the paper became a young black man walking through the door. However, William was unruffled and gave me a chance. He gave me a chance to experience what I thought I was supposed to want at the time.

He showed me I didn't have to be apprehensive in interacting with people who were different from me. In the office it wasn't just him. Most of the employees were white and I never felt any awkwardness from them. They seemed to be excited about me being in the office and they offered to help me all the time. They invited me to lunch with them. I joined in conversations that were a little outside my box, but they would clue me in. They showed me a different aspect of society for two summers and I truly appreciate them for that. Without that experience, I may have continued on my close-minded path thinking that white culture was not open to supporting the development of who I was without an agenda. It felt that these people just saw me as the next generation of themselves and wanted to do their part in my growth.

On the days I drove to work I would go train at Intensity Healthcare to train with Dr. Robert Lacy. Dr. Lacy was more than a trainer. He was a physical therapist, chiropractor, supplement specialist, and mentor. Many professional athletes worked with Dr. Lacy, and this was the first time I had ever experienced what it truly looked like to be a pro. This opportunity allowed me to see what the next level looked like. Not only did Dr. Lacy challenge me but the environment challenged me. Doctor Lacey's athletes showed me the intensity needed to be in their place. They showed me the do's and don'ts of being a professional. They told me their stories of how they got to where they were. It was like I was in school. I loved this school.

There was so much positivity swirling around me. Between my internship and working with Dr. Lacy, I believed the vision I saw for myself was on my horizon. Of course, someone felt my joy and tried to trip me up. Coach Vincent found a way to dig into my heart and try to disrupt the flow from 300 miles away.

One day walking to the train after work. Coach Vincent called me. We exchanged simple pleasantries, but I was waiting for the punchline. I already knew A&T had gone out and signed 5 freshman receivers in their 2008 recruiting class. To me that was a sign that they didn't have any plans for me, but I didn't care. I was ready to fight again for mine.

"You know we signed a bunch of receivers this year, right?" Coach Vincent said.

"Yea." I responded.

"Derek Gould, the kid from New Jersey wants #5." He stated.

"I'm #5" I responded,

"I know. We are changing your number." He said.

"What? To what number?" I asked.

"89, I think." He responded.

He added that because Derek was on scholarship, he asked for #4, but it was taken by another scholarship athlete. In my mind I thought, "#5 is taken too!" But what I said was

"So, you are going to take the jersey I earned right off my back?"

"That's just how it is." he responded.

I saw myself as the next Doug Brown. I was supposed to rock the #5 running through the tunnel, scoring touchdowns, and getting enshrined in the Hall of Fame wearing that #5. That number was mine. I earned it! Life rarely ever goes exactly the way we plan though. From that conversation, the fire inside me began to roar. I developed hate in my heart that summer. I hated Marcus Vincent and I hated Derek Gould. I hated the 5 receivers they brought in.

Hate is a terrible emotion to harbor in your heart, but what if the pure energy is harnessed in a productive direction? What we can't do is hold on to hate in its generic form. It will tear at us and hold us from our greatest potential. It will attach itself to the mind and will eventually begin to deteriorate it. We have to learn how to utilize the energy and release the feeling by putting it into our work and constructive communication. Holding on to it is like pulling the pin to a grenade and not throwing it. You have the energy in your hand, but if you don't release it, the only person to be blown up will be you. A little aggression is plenty ok, but use the energy. Don't let it fester.

That phone conversation pushed me all summer to keep all five of the freshmen on the bench. I remembered that call when I didn't feel like running that hill or moving that weight. Motivation is everywhere. I was going to know more than them. I was going to make more plays in practice than they did. I had to go harder than they did in the weight room. I had to do better than them in the classroom. There was no money invested in my future, so I had to invest in my own. I did not have the privilege of letting up. I had to be better across the board to even be considered. This sounds like something that could be discussed in a societal forum if you look deep enough into it, but we will let it lie for now.

That even playing field thing doesn't exist. Someone will always have an advantage. It can be genetic, experiential, relational, or historical. Understanding it will allow us to see where we stand in the current moment. Awareness of your current status will enable you to plan and maneuver through reality.

Sometimes our feelings may pose another obstacle to the Spartan Race of life. When we learn to manage our emotions, we will be able to not only pull up to the table but also turn the table in our favor. Can you feel your emotions? The power of those emotions multiplied by your growing experience will create exponential opportunities. Be aware of your power. Harness your power. Unleash your power!

CHAPTER 19 - REALITIES VISION

Coming off the second of back- to- back winless seasons, and holding tight to the nation's longest losing streak, the morale was somehow astronomical. Those of us still around felt we were going to change the stigma around A&T football. The streets were talking. There was talking in the barbershop, in the restaurants, on campus and in the churches. Everyone was talking trash about us. We understood where we were. We realized we were in a place where it couldn't get any worse. We began to work like we had nothing to lose. We improved in personnel, schemes, abilities, cohesiveness, and mental resilience.

As camp started the position battles ignited. We were trying to beat the next man in everything. I don't think we consciously realized that each one of us working to outshine the next guy was actually sharpening the unit as a whole. If your best is better than my best on this day, I must come back and be better than my best the next day to have a chance to survive. When the individuals battle the team is better off.

It was amazing to see the difference a year made for us. I even began to appreciate the freshman, for their talents now standing three strong. Two of the original five were deemed academically ineligible before we even made it to camp. Remember, "the way to the field is through the classroom."

Football camp is a disintegrating monster that grows and grows every passing day. College was more mentally and physically demanding than high school, as I found out my first year. That fact is what begins to weigh on most young players. I was that much more prepared than my competition, because of my tragic high school experience. As the days began to get long, bodies began to wear down. I began to separate myself. When players began to skip ice baths after practice, I found my way in every day. When soda and Kool-Aid were filling up cups at meals, mine only saw H2O. When guys were trying to sneak away from campus to find some girls. I snuck off to my room to study and get some rest. Lame right?

Football, like life, is a demanding journey. To succeed in life just as in football we have to respect the grind. Your mind and your body are your instruments to success. If neither of them is working at maximum capacity when you're in the trenches head to head with the person who wants your job, wants your position, or wants your scholarship, you are in position to lose. The person working at optimal capacity will outlast, outwork, and overcome over time. That's exactly what happened to much of the team, not only the freshman.

Though certain guys began to separate themselves from the crowd, we as a team did not have the mental resilience we thought we did to maintain the intensity that camp started off with. This lack of mental strength would be foresight to the struggles we would face as a team during the season.

LEGACY

Before the season started, we had a meeting that seemed to be intended to hone the teams focus for the journey we were about to take. During the meeting I believed the coaches failed at grasping our focus and unifying our desires. The meeting failed at delivering the jolt of energy it was intended to supply to a team who hadn't won a game in two years.

It failed until the newly appointed athletic director, Wheeler Brown, took the podium. Mr. Brown was a heavy-set man, who wore slightly tinted glasses halfway down his nose. I had never spoken to him but had seen him around practice riding his golf cart. He seemed to always be dressed in a suit no matter the weather. He spoke slowly but his voice was strong and melodic.

He introduced himself to the team and proceeded to tell us how disappointed he was in where the program had fallen. He told us that he was an old school Aggie alum who played back in the 70's with Coach Rags. He said the heart was gone from the program and that no one feared playing A&T. He was right in his views, but of course as players we didn't receive the message very well. Mr. Brown didn't care about feelings. He came to help us honestly see who we were in the mirror. Remember when you know who you are right now you can more efficiently move forward to who you want to be.

At the end of his speech is when he caught and held my full attention for years. He asked the team what the word legacy meant. Three guys took a shot at defining the word, but none seemed to say exactly what he was looking for.

"Legacy is what you leave behind" he said.

"What will they remember about your time as an Aggie? What will you leave for the Aggies that follow?"

Silence covered the room as everyone pondered what their answers to these questions would be. As I sat there, I thought of Doug Brown. The effect he had on me just because I knew what he did for this program. I thought about leaving as a MEAC champion. I thought of being the catalyst for a dynasty in Greensboro. This question touched me deeper than I believe he intended, but maybe that was the genius in his question. Asking what we wanted the end to look like, caused us to evaluate the decisions we made today.

Take a second. Think about it. Whatever you're in, and wherever you are in life, what do you want your legacy to be? What will they say about you when you are out of that space? Will the future feel a positive impact from your presence when you are gone?

CHAPTER 20 - NOT SO FAST GRASSHOPPER

I ran onto the field. A place I had only experienced from the outside looking in. I was on a college football field on game day, in front of Aggie nation. My first play as a college athlete was on the kickoff return team. For some reason, they thought it was a good idea to place me on the return team, not as a returner, but as a blocker. On the other side of the ball stood Johnson C. Smith, a D-II school from Charlotte, NC. Funny enough, lined up directly across from me was a high school teammate of mine, Jarvis Beach. He was one of the many receivers I played behind. When I saw him, he represented Westlake High School, the place I felt had tried to snuff out my ember in its infantile stages. I saw him as my last battle against my past to truly overcome that piece of my life. It was almost like a rite of passage to be sure I was ready to move on.

With the boom of Eric's foot hitting the ball, my college football clock started. This year was different. All the work and preparation seemed to have us ready for this first test. The plan was to run the ball and that's precisely what we did. Michael Ferguson went for 100 yards and his backup went for 92. It was over before it started.

#1

It was third and 10, as we were driving to put points on the board before halftime. I knew my route, I saw the defense, and I knew I should get the ball. As I came out of my break on my curl route I saw it spiraling through the air, with the white stripe yelling at me in morse code. Our quarterback had given me a gift that I had waited a year for. My hands reached out and latched on securing my first collegiate reception. Turning up the field I could see the end zone. It wasn't far. However, there was one defender between me and an epic climax. Making my move he jumped to one side opening a lane to the end zone. Bursting forward it went through my mind. My first catch is going to be a touchdown. Just as I went to lunge for the goal line, I felt the defender I thought I had gotten rid of grab hold of my leg and drop all of his weight on my lower body. Not strong enough to handle the resistance he added, we both went crashing down. When I looked up, I was so close. I was lying on the three-yard line, only 9 feet from the promised land.

Just when you think you have arrived, reality hits you with the Mutombo finger wag. "Not so fast, grasshopper."

There are many lessons to be learned before you can have it all. I thought I had been through enough and challenged enough to overcome one defender. I thought it was my time to cross the goal line for the first touchdown of my life. Obviously, it wasn't. Obviously, I had more work to do, but I was so close. As I found out during the season, I was still so far away.

We scored on the next play and went on to win big. Ending the longest losing streak in the nation at 27 games and sparking a buzz around Aggie Nation. The turnaround of the program had begun, and we were going to be the catalyst.

We went into the next week on an emotional high. Not did we win, we dominated. We executed and we had fun doing it. We carried that high on into another one of our in-state rivals, the dangerous Winston Salem State University.

It wasn't as pretty as the JCSU game, but we found a way to win. I wasn't starting, but I was getting considerable playing time. I wasn't making a whole bunch of big plays, but the experience of being out there would prove invaluable. In the early stages of any path you take, experience trumps all as long as you grow from the experiences. Success or failure doesn't matter, get the knowledge.

HERE WE GO AGAIN

Winning definitely feels good. So good that you can forget you were just 0-27 two weeks ago. Of course, "We drank the Kool-Aid," but in week 3 we realized it was a little watered down.

We bussed everywhere we played. When Norfolk State showed up on the schedule, we hopped on the road for 4 hours. It was a close game and we pulled within 6 points going into the 4th quarter. However, that mental fatigue that we talked about earlier showed itself. We put up a goose egg in the fourth quarter. Our inexperience in winning and our vast experience in losing caused us to revert back to the mindset we knew so well.

"Here we go again!"

When you are new to succeeding, it's easy to fall back into old losing ways. We have to continue the positive self-talk and promotion. Most importantly we have to continue intense preparation and focus. If you don't, you'll end up allowing the doubt and "here we go again" syndrome to conquer. Once that ounce of doubt crept back in, it infected our entire team including the coaching staff. We began to spiral out of control. Week after week, loss after loss, we fell into more and more pieces. Not having the mental fortitude and resilience engrained throughout our team caused one lousy play to turn into one bad drive. That bad drive turned into one bad game and spiraled into another lousy season.

Negative occurrences are going to happen, it's inevitable. It is up to each of us individually to take a stand in response to these occasions and say, "This is not going to break me." We can lean on each other but once each individual is fortified in their own mind then we can take it to the level that wins games. "This is not going to break us."

We did not have this mentality as a team. All this team knew was losing. The last generation of Aggie champions were extinct in our locker room. We were running around the bottom of the bucket with all our tools, but no one knew how to build a ladder. It would take an experienced leader to reach in and show us the way. That hand was a few years away.

CHAPTER 21 - WELCOME TO COLLEGE

FOOTBALL

Throughout my first year playing college football, I had many significant first. I played my first game, caught my first pass, and started my first game. The biggest first had to be my first touchdown. It was a simple two yard slant route. I acted a plum fool, celebrating like I had never caught a touchdown before. Well, not one of my twelve catches in high school went for a touchdown. So, it actually was the first touchdown of my life. No one understood I had been dreaming of this moment since I was four years old.

This was my fourth year playing football. All the work I had put in to just have the opportunity to continue playing. All those hours in the gym, on the field, studying, sacrificing, hurting, and failing. When I finally carried the ball across the threshold of the goal line there was an eruption of emotion. That is the part of football that is addictive. That is the part of any passionate work that is addictive. Success is seen in the moment, but it's earned over thousands of unseen moments. Crossing the goal line is celebration worthy.

Now remember this. Enjoy the moment as you should, but always remember that the game, the season, and your journey is not over. Keep the ultimate goal in mind in your celebration. Problems arise when you get lost in the passing moments and don't maintain your focus.

All my firsts were the highlights of that season, but one of my low lights literally lifted me even higher than any of those highlights. We had driven 14 hours up to Dover, Delaware to play Delaware State University. Early in the game we were trying to establish some offensive momentum, because that was something we consistently lacked.

GET LIFTED

Coach called a trick play, a hook and lateral. The play was designed for the quarterback to drop back and throw the ball to one of my teammates. As this is happening, it was my job to slowly run across the field toward my teammate as he caught the ball. After he secures the catch, he is supposed to pitch it to me. This allows me to catch the defense by surprise and scamper down the sideline for a touchdown. In practice, it worked every time. It was an excellent plan for Delaware State's defense. But, as we all know, plans do not always go as planned.

On this particular day and on this particular play, the receiver intended to catch the pass got jammed up at the line. As our quarterback, now Shelton Morgan, dropped back the offensive line allowed pressure in his face. This forced Shelton to scramble out of the pocket. As I ran across the field, I saw all of this unfolding. Instinctively, I began waving my hands at my QB. In his desperation he let it fly as he was about to get mauled.

When your quarterback gives you a chance, you have to "GO GET IT!" You have to make a play. You have to make everyone on the field and in the coaches' box look good. I fearlessly elevated as if I was the only one on the field. I snagged it and posed for the poster-worthy image of me soaring into the clouds. That moment quickly passed as I started my descent. The reality was I wasn't the only one on the field. I turned my head looking for where I was going to land, expecting to take off down the sideline. What I saw was not the green grass I expected. What I saw was the red and white of a Delaware State helmet.

The next thing I remember was getting helped off the ground with the ball still tucked away under my arm, with no idea how I got on the ground. As my teammates helped me to my feet, I saw the trainers were halfway on the field. When they saw me stand up, they stopped. They asked me if I was good to keep playing.

"Yea I'm good" I said woozy and dazed.

But for some reason, I ran off the field. When I got to the sideline coach asked me if I was ok. My response this time was different,

"No, my head is hurting",

By now my head was hurting. My back had started to throb but instead of staying on the sideline to get checked out, for some reason I ran back on the field. I was all discombobulated. When I got to the huddle, my teammates asked me the same question. I could see in their eyes they were amazed I was even awake. I still had no clue what happened. The trainer did the right thing and saved me from myself by pulling me off the field.

I later found out from watching film that I had been hit helmet to helmet by one of their linebackers. My body responded by completing a full back flip. I landed on my hip, then my back, and ended with my head slamming into the ground. To this day I have not seen anything like it.

The trainers took me to the bench to conduct a concussion test. When they took my helmet off, one of my teammates standing near burst into laughter and yelled: "Damn bro, you go snot in both your eyebrows." I had literally gotten the snot knocked out of me. At this moment, my head was still ringing. My neck and hip were stinging. I had one of the moments where I had to ask myself, do you really want to do this? I had never been in so much pain in so many different places at one time. We were a losing program, and the future didn't look any brighter. I wasn't on scholarship, so I was paying to get hit like this.

"Is this really what you want to do with your life?"

I passed every part of the concussion evaluation.

"Do you want to go back in the game?" the trainers looked at me and asked.

"Yes!" I replied. I was answering her question, but I was also answering my own as well.

The dizziness was dissipating, and things were beginning to become clear again. I felt that all I wanted from this game far outweighed this temporary discomfort. I put my helmet back on and walked up to the offensive coordinator and told him "whenever you're ready coach". Eventually I got back in the game, but it didn't help much. We went on to lose badly.

After the game, I met 20 of my family members who had come from Baltimore, Philadelphia, and Atlanta to support me. They told me that they hadn't even sat down before they witnessed "the hit". People that really support you always have a perspective that keeps you strong in your battles. When I came to the sideline, my teammates were either worried or laughing at me which were expected reactions. My family continued to harp on, "But you held on to the ball!" The catch was only for 5 yards, but they saw a more significant lesson. That's what family does. When you are broken down they run to your aid and help support you, to help you finish the race. They helped me understand that no matter how hard you get hit going after whatever your thing is, hold on to it. When your head stops spinning, and the dust clears it will still be in your grasp. Hold tight to what you want in this life, through the bumps, bruises, and maybe even a possible concussion.

TIDES OF CHANGE

The last time I ever saw Bob Mason was getting off the 14 hour bus ride after that loss. Just as I had been knocked for a painful loop our entire program would be knocked into disarray. Our head coach, the leader of our ranks, was fired after that game. The comfortable seat we had all gotten accustomed to, was abruptly pulled from beneath us by the omen of change. Most of my teammates were recruited by these coaches. Some of us only knew these coaches. The idea of new coaches, new systems, new philosophies, and new people was unnerving.

We finished the season off with Coach Rags as the interim head coach. We loved Rags and even rallied around him to win our next game, but we were not able to make any real steps up the mountain, finishing the season 3-9. We all knew the sea of change was upon us.

CHAPTER 22 - THE PROPHECY

My family normally heads back to the land that took my uncles life, Baltimore, MD, for Thanksgiving. It's a time that we reflect on what we are thankful for and an opportunity to fellowship in our village of love. We all gather at my grandmother's house to partake in a feast that was lick the plate kind of good.

The biggest force that I felt during this time of the year was my connection to the roots of my family. I heard stories of those who had passed away and of those who were still with us in their younger days. It gave me the opportunity to understand where this part of me was built.

At this point in my life, I was 19 years old, the same age my uncle was when he was taken from this earth. Knowing this I felt a sense of honor to have carried his name this far, but I also felt I wanted others to honor and respect his name. In the mental space I was in, I could only see one result that intersected that goal with my passion. Putting our name in the record books.

I had gotten my hands on an A&T media guide before I left for the break. In the very back were the A&T all-time records. All the A&T legends littered the top of each statistical category. In all the receiving categories one name was constant, Herbert Harbison.

The night before Thanksgiving I stayed up late obsessing over the records. Calculating averages, evaluating where certain guys were in certain parts of their career, and how far behind I was on the journey to the book. After a couple hours I came up with what my stats would be next season.

Thanksgiving Day, my dad and I went to the gym and on the way back we parked up the block from my grandmother's house. I had been contemplating telling him what I had come up with. As we walked down the surprisingly quiet block, we began talking A&T football, hypothesizing what was going to happen with the team. I felt this was the time and place to share the results of my journey down the rabbit hole the previous night. With no set up for where I was about to take the conversation, I interjected.

"Dad, next year I am going to get 70 receptions, over 1000 yards, and 10 TDs."

I knew this would put me in position to become the all-time leader in many categories by the time I graduated.

Expecting him to react excitedly, I was thoroughly disappointed in his reaction. He looked at me with a smirk.

"OK, show me!" He said.

"I will!" I shot back irritated and burning inside.

We didn't say another word about it as we walked into my grandmother's house of love. What I had just done was put myself out there. I had invited my support system to be my accountability system.

Even if my family never said anything to me about what my goals were, when I looked at them, it forced me to look at me. Was I being a man of my word or had I just been spewing sounds of no substance? That is why my dad didn't react. Anyone can just say what they are going to do. Until you put down the video game controllers, get off the dusty couch, put in the work and the time to reach your goal, what reason is there to get excited? Are you truly "bout dat action?" or "do you talk a big game? Everything we earn in this life takes action to attain. Ideas and planning are key elements to attaining a dream but without action they are as real as a unicorn. Not the Porzingis kind of unicorn, for all you smart alecks. We are talking about the one with the horn and rainbows that runs around with glitter flying everywhere.

When is the last time you have seen one of those running in the wild?

It is a major step of vulnerability to open up to another person about your goals. It is a symbol of trust to offer your dreams to another person's awareness. You give them permission to hold you accountable for your actions as you move forward in life. Even if they never say a word, you know they know. Your honor and self-respect are now at risk if you quit. This book that you are reading right now was pushed along partly because I told certain people that I was going to do it. Every time I saw or spoke to one of these people, I thought about what I needed to do to finish this book. What I needed to do to be a man of my own word. Some never said a word. Some called in and checked on me. Either way their presence made me evaluate what I needed to do next to put this book in your hands.

I encourage you all to find someone that you trust and tell them your greatest aspiration. That moment of truth will also heighten your relationship and your connection. It's like entering into a covenant. If you are on the receiving end, honor this covenant. Another being, be it your child, sibling, mentee, employee, or friend has entrusted you with a piece of their heart. Treat it as such!

CHAPTER 23 - CHANGE

There is a book titled *Who Moved My Cheese* by Dr. Spencer Johnson. This book can be looked at from different perspectives. One way to look at it is the process people go through as they react to change. The experienced traveler may move through the steps a little more quickly than the novice, but the steps are always in play.

I'll let you get the book and read it on your own. But briefly, it depicts four characters, two little people named Hem and Haw, and two rats named Sniff and Scurry. At one point during the story, the goal -the cheese these characters achieve disappears and they are confronted with a drastic change. Sniff and Scurry are ready and don't waste much time moving on in search of their next goal. They transitioned so fast it was almost as if they saw the change coming. Eventually, they find their next success. Meanwhile, Hem and Haw mentally get stuck in the place where they had grown comfortable hoping the success, the cheese would come back to them.

Hem is totally against the change. He whines, complains, and yells out in frustration. Haw, on the other hand, is initially resistant to the change because it presents the unknown. Eventually he begins to realize he is stuck in place and he starts to play with the thought of venturing out past where his comfort currently resides. One day he leaves Hem to complain by himself and steps out into the unknown. On his journey he begins to have several realizations that start to strengthen and grow who he is as a person. Haw gradually becomes more comfortable searching out his new cheese until he eventually joins Sniff and Scurry in newfound success. Hem was never seen again, because he got stuck and did not accept that change was uncomfortable but necessary.

Change is inevitable and necessary in all of our lives. It's human nature to want to resist change. Being born we go through a dramatic change. We hem and haw and cry until literal exhaustion. We are born into change and the first lesson we learn is adapting to it. With each shift in life we encounter, we must understand how we react to the change. As we move through life we must learn from each transition. Eventually when we are met with change we can move through hemming and hawing much quicker. We can move on to sniffing out the remedy and scurrying to it.

Change is extremely uncomfortable initially. Your first reaction may be to rebel and stick to your routine. What I have learned is that adapting to change will, at the very least, stretch your ability to handle change in the future. Change will require you to learn new skills that will prepare you for some situation in your immediate or far reaching future. Opportunities to change are opportunities to get comfortable being uncomfortable. When you can understand what that feels like, nothing can stop you on your journey.

CHANGING OF THE GUARD

When the spring semester hit, it came with significant changes. We were introduced to a brand-new coaching staff. This concept was nerve-racking. I spent the previous year and a half attempting to impress and earn the trust of one set of coaches just to have to start all over again.

Coach Howard Thomas came in after holding the defensive coordinator position at Mississippi Valley State University. He brought with him a brand-new coaching staff, a brand new mentality, and a brand new philosophy. He brought with him "change."

From the first meeting, Coach Thomas and his staff were a drastic change for A&T football. We realized this was a whole new environment. He was the complete opposite of Coach Mason. It was like trading in a fluffy puppy for a lion.

Coach Thomas was from the tough streets of Philadelphia, PA. He imposed the intensity he developed through football and his upbringing in his interactions. I always wanted to see Coach Thomas put on some pads and set practice off in an Oklahoma drill. He had that kind of mentality and presence. When spring ball began, the tempo was faster, more intense, and more competitive. Combined with learning new systems on both sides of the ball, this staff delighted in creating a chaotic environment challenging us to adapt to sudden change.

I took this challenge as an opportunity to establish my position on a relatively leveled playing field now that the previous regime's bias was out the door. Everyone did not respond to this challenge in a positive light. This was seen especially in those who had previously been beneficiaries of the inherent bias created when a coach decides to invest his fate and the school's money into an 18-year-old kid.

Some people are naturally talented to perform specific skills. But the old saying "Hard work beats talent when talent doesn't work hard" reigns true. Many of my teammates had never faced any adversity in the realm of football because they had always been the favorite or the star. There were a few of them who rebelled. TV and movies depict rebelling against a new regime resulting in exile or worse. Coach Thomas and crew abided by the same philosophy. He dismissed multiple players from the program. Walk-ons and scholarship athletes alike. No one was safe.

It's funny how some situations that seem troubling while you're in the midst can add exponential value to your life. They help by preparing you for something in your future that you never see coming. My struggles in high school to play football actually prepared me for the current playing field. I was ready for the adversity. It allowed me to remain and increase my focus. Your problems today are preparing you for your opportunities tomorrow.

In my mind, I knew it was now or never. I knew my folks were running low on the funds they had saved for me to go to college. I was going to have to take out a student loan or transfer to another school closer to home. My parents taught me how detrimental debt can be. That's why I wanted a scholarship so badly, to finally give my parents a financial break and leave school not owing anyone anything was added timber to my fire.

EVERYTHING AFFECTS EVERYTHING

My focus on the field began to affect my performance in the classroom. I still had a passing GPA, but I began contemplating hanging my cleats up. I loved the game, but I knew how important my education was. I didn't want to half-ass on the field, but I also knew I couldn't half-ass in the classroom. I would get left behind in one or both. To succeed in my degree, you had to be wholly consumed in the culture of engineering. Just showing up and passing was a thing of the past. Electrical engineering, the study of electricity is very theoretical. Understanding the theoretical concepts required massive amounts of real time and effort to grasp. As a direct effect of time being allocated to school I thought less time would be left for football. In my heart, I wasn't ready to be done with football.

With all the changes happening on the football field, the focus I had previously maintained in the classroom began to falter. I was always able to show up for workouts and grind them out, handle practice, class and studying. At this time, I was so focused on this opportunity to earn a scholarship and solidify my position that my academic success began to fall by the wayside. When you don't intentionally manage all of your priorities something inevitably doesn't receive the attention it deserves.

By the time workouts, class, labs, meetings, 7 on 7, practice, and studying my plays was over, I didn't put near enough energy into studying for my course load. The domino effect of our coaching change and the opportunity I was running after resulted in me failing the first class in my entire life, Differential Equations. I also got a D in another. I started to choose the gym over homework. I chose sleep and recovery over class. I studied film and my playbook over studying for school. Academically this was the worst semester I had ever completed in my life because my focus was elsewhere. My current priorities muddied the end goal of why I was even in school to begin with.

As I realized I was not handling the change in my life very well I decided to get back to what really seems to hone my focus and efforts. I began to pray consistently again. I reached back and watched *The Secret* again. I continually thought and spoke positively. I communicated to the power of the universe daily. I opened my heart and mind to peace. All the while I continued working like a walk-on. I earned every opportunity to strap on my helmet, but now I was able to manage my scholastic responsibilities better.

How do you adapt to change? Do you adapt the same way in every area of your life? Bruce Lee said it better than it's ever been said. "Be like water." Be able to adapt to change, able to mold into any form, but retain your ultimate strength."

CHAPTER 24 - $$$PEAK IT!

Success normally comes where your focus resides. I saw the coaching change as an opportunity and a gap in the structure of the program to earn the scholarship I wanted so badly. I literally had money on the brain. When spring practice started, the coaches put tape across all of our helmets with our names on it. I wanted them to know me, but I also didn't want any misunderstanding about what I was out there to get. I took my own piece of tape and placed it over the tape with my name on it. Instead of my name, I put a line from the 2001 comedy *How High*. I wrote "I NEED $$$" across the forehead of my helmet. Our new receiver coach, Tyrone Powell, thought I was playing around, and he joked with me about it for a day or two. After a few practices, he realized that I was dead serious. It showed in my play, preparation, and my tone. He knew I was "bout dat action." He started calling me "I NEED MONEY". He kept me accountable whenever it seemed the focus of my goal was slipping.

Soon he began to give me daily reminders: "Remember what you're after! Remember what you want!" I never forgot and I pushed the limits. A couple more fights ensued, a lot of plays were made, and respect across the board increased. I wanted it bad and that symbol on the front of my helmet spoke to me every day. It spoke to the man next to me in the huddle. It spoke to the man that lined up in front of me. It told them there are no days off. There are no plays off. There are no reps off because there is a reason behind everything I do.

The reason wasn't the money in it of itself. The reason was the tuition weighing on my parents. The reason was my financial future. The reason was to be an example to the younger members of my family. The reason was my academic future. The reason was because they told me the belief I had in myself was too lofty. The reason was they took the jersey off my back and expected me to fold. The reason was to look myself in the mirror and one day become who I saw. When you line up with the right why is why's branded across your heart and mind, no resistance will be able to outlast your determination and drive.

We ended the spring with the blue and gold game. It was our inter squad scrimmage where everything that we learned from our new coaching staff over the previous 3 months was put on display. I redshirted a season and now had a season under my belt. This was my coming out party. I scored two touchdowns, showing the team they could trust me. They could come to me. My spring performance left an imprint on the minds of my teammates as well as our new coaches. The extra time, focus, and effort literally was about to pay off.

SIGNING DAY

During one of our team meetings following the spring game, Coach Thomas called a list of names. My name being one of them. Trying to get a bead on what was going on I tried to find out what the list was for. I couldn't put together the correlation of the guys he was calling. Each person went up and signed a piece of paper. When it was my turn to sit across from him, I was still unaware of what was going on. He looked at me and growled.

"Umm hmm Mr. Wallace, you have shown us a lot this spring. We have decided that we are going to put you on partial scholarship."

My eyes widened; my heart started thumping. I tried to keep my cool because I was in front of all of my teammates, but I guarantee they all could tell what was going on inside of me. Then it hit me. All those guys that signed before me were on scholarship. They were renewing their scholarships and I was being inducted partially into their ranks. Speak it, work it, and it will be.

I was signing what thirteen of my high school teammates signed two years prior, as I sat in the crowd jealous. I felt what they must have been feeling when they were signing the dotted line. Funny how IT might not happen when you want it to. But if you chase IT relentlessly with your whole heart, you'll find your way to IT at some point and in some way.

This accomplishment reaffirmed the work I had been putting in. It affirmed that I was part of the plan going forward with this team. It reminded me that I was becoming what only I had originally believed. This accomplishment made that old time saying: "When you put your mind to it, anything is possible" become fact in my mind. This moment relieved some of the burdens my education posed on my parents and put more of the responsibility of my future in my own hands. The weight of that $18,732 per year tuition was cut in half.

As a redshirt freshman, I started my first college game. I caught my first touchdown, led the team in receptions, somehow voted receiver of the year, and earned a partial scholarship. As I was on the highway back home to Atlanta for the summer heading into my sophomore campaign, all I could think was "Let's get more!"

HALFTIME

CHAPTER 25 - MILT STEGALL UNIVERSITY

In life you will find that people come in and out of your life. Some enhance you, while some test you. It is up to us as individuals to absorb the positive and learn from it while we shrug off the negative. One of the true turning points in my life came in the form of a relationship that blossomed out of the effort I gave as a youth.

To this day without a shadow of a doubt, I believe that my crossing paths with Milt Stegall was that universal *Law of Attraction* working in a subtle but drastic way to change my life. Milt Stegall is the greatest receiver and maybe the greatest player in CFL (Canadian Football League) history. He played 14 seasons in Winnipeg, Manitoba for the Blue Bombers and amassed 147 touchdowns. The nickname the G.O.A.T (Greatest of All Time) is thrown around a lot these days, but Milt is one of those shooting stars whom that title rests easily upon with no debate.

It just so happened that Milt had a young son named Chase who was 4 years old. Chase played soccer for the best soccer coach I ever played for. Coach Keith Frazier coached me throughout middle school where I saw the most development in my soccer abilities. He made me work harder than I ever worked on my technical skills, my physicality, and my mentality. He challenged me to be a leader. He challenged me to rise. It was only right that he would be the catalyst to the next level of my development, even if it was on a completely different field. Coach Keith stayed in contact with my dad over the years, as he had always taken an interest in my growth.

Once Coach Keith realized who the father of one of his players was, he put the plot in motion. He contacted my dad and between the 3 of them they set me up to work out with Milt. This was the best / worst thing that could have happened to me.

FIND A WAY

Nervously I made my way to the birthplace of my football career, Westlake High School, where I was to meet Milt at 10:00 AM one Saturday morning. I rolled up precisely at 10 o'clock, but that meant I didn't get to the field until 10:03am. He was there early, warming up on his own. I thought he was going to be this huge imposing figure. Milt stands about 5'11, 180 pounds, but he is a cyborg, half man half machine. Even at 50 years old he is still in excellent playing shape. You can randomly show up to a track in Southwest Atlanta and you may see a bald guy running 300 meter sprints full tilt, doing sets of 100 pushups, some ridiculous ab routine, and then just walk off the field like he was finishing his evening stroll. Seeing him warming up I thought "This old man is ready, ain't he."

"You're late, I'm going to teach you how to be punctual, sucka." was the first thing he said. The second thing he said to me was a question. "What do you catch the ball with?"

"My hands!" I said confidently.

"Wrong," he said. "Try again!"

I looked at him like he was crazy because of course you catch the ball with your hands. I decided to play his little game. I wasn't going to be stumped on such a simple question.

"Uhhhhh your fingertips" I said,

"Wrong" again he said. "Try again?"

" Your Brain?"

"Wrong" he said.

Now I thought he was playing with me. He just wanted to see if I was confident. I said my original answer, believing he would concede that he wanted me to stand behind my answer.

"My hands?" I said.

"You already said that!" he said.

He had the football in his hands throughout this entire back and forth. I was stumped. He told me to back up, which I did. Then he told me to catch the ball. He threw it and I did. By this time, I was extremely confused because the answer obviously had to be hands, because I just showed him. I threw the ball back to him. As he was about to wind up and throw the ball again, he told me "Now close your eyes."

"Yep, he's crazy" I said in my head.

I'm pretty crazy myself because I did it thinking some sort of Spidey sense I never knew about was going to kick in. Once my eyelids shut, fear began to creep in because I thought he could hit me square in my face or in the nuts. How could I catch the ball if I couldn't see it? It was at that moment; the answer hit me square in the face.

"Your eyes." I said opening my eyes.

"Right, now we can begin" He grinned.

Before we continue, I want you to take a deeper look at that metaphor. You catch the ball with your eyes. The ball is the goals you set in your life. Your goals are only attainable if you see them. Visualization creates reality.

"Your imagination is everything.

It is the preview of life's

coming attractions."

~ Albert Einstein

Meaning if you see and envision what you want in this world, it can make its way into your life. You just have to put yourself in position to catch it. See even Einstein new *The Secret.* If you go through this world with your eyes closed and without vision, there is no way you will catch the ball.

After he dropped that intellectual gem on me, we proceeded to do a warmup that lasted about 10 minutes but felt like I had just done an hour-long road race. There was no way that I was going to make it through the next 50 minutes. In that initial session, we did plyometrics, ladder drills, cone drills, ran routes, catching drills, conditioning, and a core workout. He put me through every pace that I had ever known and some I had never been through before.

I was so relieved when we finished the last drill. I sat on the bench and guzzled what was left of my gallon of water. That's when he hit me with:

"Naw, we aren't done yet. Now I'm going to teach you not to be late, sucka!"

My heart skipped two beats just to get itself back on rhythm. He pulled out an elastic harness that connected me to him.

"You get to taste the Equalizer." He told me.

I had to pull him the length of the football field. Once I got to the end, I was to step out of the harness and run back to the other end where I started. As I strapped in and looked down to the end of the field, it seemed to be a mile away.

"GO" Milt shouted.

I took off digging with everything I had thinking I was going to pull him out of his shoes. Milt pretty much sat down on the other end of the elastic strap and it felt like I was dragging a car. Normally 100 yards takes about 11-14 seconds. It took me 60 pulling him on my back. The harder I pulled it seemed the harder he resisted. I could feel my legs, core, and breath leaving me. Everything was heavy and I still had 25 yards to go. Somehow, I crossed the goal line and collapsed. All the pain seemed like it was waiting for me to finish as it rushed to every part of my legs as they began to throb and seize up. Gasping for every breath I rolled over on the ground, eyes closed. From above me, Milt yelled,

"Get up now you have to run back to the other end."

"How?" went through my mind.

Staggering to my feet, I leaned forward and just prayed my feet would react and move forward too. As I started to go, Milt yelled:

"I'm going to give you a 25-yard head start. Don't let me catch you!"

I found some energy from somewhere and gave all of that. I couldn't allow this old man to run me down with a 25-yard head start.

All the energy I found was not enough. He caught me with about 15 yards left. The gorilla that hopped on my back weighed me down to a slugs pace. When I finally crossed the goal line, I collapsed again. My body completely locked up. All I could do was crawl and roll around in agony. At some point, I figured just lying there on the ground not moving was the best move for me. Milt jokingly but seriously stated,

"I bet you won't be late again huh, sucka."

As you can see, he tends to use that 1970's disco lingo for his insults. I was in so much pain I didn't know what to do. He then felt the need to disclose that he would work up to doing 6 of those before every season and that is when he knew he was ready to go to camp. And with that he just walked off the field.

Milt left and I was still laying on the field by myself. I had never felt like this in my life. I was physically destroyed and mentally depleted. When I finally mustered the energy to stumble to my car, I sat back and reflected on the last hour of my life. A very weird sensation came over me. I was afraid but excited at the same time. Afraid to go back out there with him and risk feeling like this again. Excited because I knew no one on my team would be close to me if I continued to work with Milt. I believed that the vision I created of myself would truly be attainable if I stuck with Milt, no matter how much it hurt. Eventually I realized that I probably couldn't feel any worse than I did at that moment and I wasn't dead. I might as well show back up for another round.

When your why is greater than the thousands of why nots, you will find a way through. My dad would say "You can find a million excuses why not; it only takes one reason to do it!" Step one will always be simply to show up. I can guarantee you will not improve if you don't show up to the opportunities to grow yourself. The lesson I learned that day was when you show up, be on time. This lesson carries over into all areas of our lives. Being punctual can tell a lot about you. It says you are professional and you are disciplined. It says you respect other people's time, and If you think about it, life is calculated in time. You show people you care about their life when you show them you care about their time. We also show people that whatever IT is, is important to us."

After that initial work out, Milt called my pops and told him that I had something. The bigger question was going to be was I willing to work to find out what that something could be. You would never have considered me the fastest. I didn't jump the highest or lift the most weight. You could have considered me a slightly above average athlete, but I had created my own talent to continue to compete. Hard work became my talent. The motto became:

"Work harder than you think they're working," and I always thought the best were working harder than me. Milt was exactly who I needed and he came exactly when I needed him.

For the remainder of my college career, I would get on the field with Milt whenever I was in Atlanta. Even when I was in summer school, I would come home on the weekends and catch two sessions with Milt. Milt was different. He wasn't just training my body; he trained my mind. His mantra was "FIND A WAY!" When the sun is beaming down on you, your body is collapsing, your breath is escaping you, your vision is blurred, he would throw a 60 yards bomb for you to adjust to and yell out "FIND A WAY!"

When you've just been fired, the mortgage is due next week, your daughter's tuition is coming up and your car just broke down. "FIND A WAY!" We don't have much time in life to feel sorry for ourselves. The team or the family, will be counting on you. In my experience with life, you are never out of the fight unless you give up. As long as you chase a solution with all your heart, a path will illuminate itself. This was the best halftime speech I could have asked for. "FIND A WAY!" Coach Keith Frazier and Milt Stegall. "THANK YOU

3RD QUARTER

CHAPTER 26 - AHHH REAL MONSTERS

After six weeks of training with Milt, I returned to A&T a new man and again with a new number. I didn't have the best relationship with the number 89, because it signified the opposite of who I was trying to be. I wanted to choose who I was. The number 89 was the number forced upon me after the number 5 was stripped from my back. As the opportunity presented itself, I chose a new number. I wanted to create my own fate. Another step toward that was choosing number 8.

The 2009 version of me was well-conditioned, technically sound, more aware, and mentally strong. I began to set myself apart from the other receivers in our 7 on 7 practices. It didn't matter who was in front of me or what coverage they were in. I was convinced I was more prepared than anyone on the field. Confidence didn't come from an internal arrogance that I was ordained to be better. It came from the work I put in to be better than me. It came from those moments I thought I was on my last breath but somehow this amazing body we have responded to my mind and found a way to push through and put out more. Real confidence is developed in the preparation. My confidence was soaring because I put in the work.

The work with Milt solidified this walk-on kicker as the number one receiver on the depth chart. But again, they brought in a couple more guys hoping they would supplant me. "Here we go again." Remember what you have gone through before. It may look a little different, but you are more prepared to go through it again. The new challenge came in the form of Jay Carter and Larry Raper, two small, but very talented athletes. Larry was the first guy that I had ever seen run a legit 4.3 with pads on. Jay had suction cups for hands and made Odell Beckham Jr. type catches before Odell was ever heard of outside of Louisiana.

As much talent as these two young guys possessed, they both possessed the same flaws. They were unfocused and immature. Eventually, we began to call them "Little Monsters," because of their antics. Neither of them took the game seriously. Since they had been showered with praise and adoration for their talents their entire lives, they felt like there was a different set of rules for them. This created frustration for the rest of us who had actually donned an A&T jersey and gone to war for the program before.

These "Little Monsters" also created an opportunity for me that I was unaware of until Coach Powell laid it out in front of me.

"These are the guys that are going to be on the field with you at some point, and we can't have them doing their own thing."

His next words hit harder than I think he intended. "You are the leader of this group. You have to show these young boys how to be student athletes and respectable young men."

Initially this was a lot of pressure. To guide two young wild boys into being responsible young men. I thought "That's not my job. I just want the other half of my scholarship!"

No doubt about it, these guys were talented. When talent has never had to work hard, being challenged can be extremely uncomfortable even when it is necessary. Team sports are called team sports because it takes a collective of individuals working together on the same page to find success. In football even a player as dynamic as Mike Vick could never play defense, get an interception, line up and run an 80-yard touchdown. Ok, because of how great Mike Vick was he might have been able to do it once but not over and over. Definitely not throughout a game let alone the whole season. All that to say, we can only be as great as the success of our teammates. The stronger your circle, the higher you rise. The higher we rise. With all the losing we had done, I realized no matter how great I thought I was I couldn't succeed if my lineman didn't block, running backs didn't run hard, quarterback couldn't throw accurately, or my fellow receivers couldn't make plays. As a leader, your success relies on how well the group does. You must develop and invest in the people around you. When we grow, we win.

I watched the little monsters reign havoc on the team throughout camp and into the season. I reached a point that I had had enough. My natural leadership style is to lead by example but dealing with them was going to have to be different. Just making plays and working hard as the example was not reaching them. I was going to have to grow in my leadership abilities. The best place to reach someone is where they are. Expecting a blind man to find you on the path is futile. As a leader you have to go to where the blind man walks. You have to gain his trust, grab him by the hand, and show him the way. Eventually, he will be able to maneuver on his own and maybe one of Jesus's many miracles will occur.

I was able to create a bit of a connection with Jay because we were both from Georgia. Even though we had different upbringings, we could talk about places we both had been and music we both grew up to. Those little connection points opened up a small crease in his rebellion, allowing me to slowly earn his respect. I was able to see where he was coming from in a lot of his actions. He was able to feel I was genuinely trying to help him grow as a player and as a man. Jay started to really turn the corner going into his second year, but a relapse of judgment got him a criminal case. This aligned with poor effort in school and his history landed him back home in Georgia. The football potential he held in both his 4XL hands was flushed down the toilet due to a moment of poor judgement.

Larry was a whole different kind of monster. He wasn't as reckless, but it was evident Larry had been the superstar for the entire town of Shelby, NC. Anytime someone asked him to do something he would rebel. Be it pouting, fussing, or being a smart ass, it was like dealing with my four-year-old nephew. He was the kid you told not to do something. Then they walk over looking at you the whole time and do whatever you told them not to do.

I vividly remember one day when it was raining and Coach Powell asked Larry to pick it up in warm-ups, but Larry was having one of his days. Coach said something to him three or four times. Larry would move slower and slower. Eventually, coach said, "If you don't want to be here you can take your pads off." Most players may have continued to carry an attitude but would have gone a little harder. That was too generic for Larry. What Larry did was unsnap his pads and flipped his helmet off which hit the ground with a thud. Then he slipped right out of his pads in one fluid motion. His pads and helmet were scattered across the ground as he walked over to the fence and posted up looking at coach. He was standing shirtless on the fence in the rain just to rebel. I couldn't believe what I had just watched. The crazy thing is I had seen guys kicked off the team let alone kicked out of practice for less. Our offensive coordinator saw the back end of the situation. He went over and animatedly talked Larry into putting his pads back on and getting into practice. Seeing things like this creates dissension in a team environment. Some people are more talented than others on the team, but remember no one is more talented than the team.

After this incident, I knew I had to reach out to Larry. Not just for his sake but for the sake of the team. Though he was acting out by himself, he was infecting the morale us all. The coaches would still play him on Saturday after something like that. When you have guys less talented, working harder to conform to the system that aren't dressing, turmoil is soon to fester. It sent a bad message throughout the locker room. To me this was the first sign that this staff could lose this team.

Reaching Larry was a bit tougher. We didn't have much in common. He was from a small town. He grew up a star and he was a father. He didn't really care about school. I was pretty stumped when it came to really connecting with Larry until his weakness opened the crease I needed. The one thing that slowed this speedster was he had trouble catching the ball and he knew it.

One day he came over to me after practice and asked me: "Can you teach me how to catch better?"

This caught me by surprise because Larry didn't ask for much. I was also honored because he thought enough of me to show a sign of vulnerability. We began to spend time after practice every day. We worked on catching the ball with his eyes, his hand placement, and body control. We started to have conversations deeper than the surface. He began to trust me, and I began to understand him.

Why would I trust you if I don't believe you have my best interest at heart? Why would I listen to you if I don't believe you have value to give me? As you grow, you will find reasons that will allow you to trust your development and vulnerabilities in the hands of another person. If you genuinely want to influence people, it is essential to connect with the person beyond your title or position.

Larry was able to become aware how destructive his behavior was. We became real friends and real brothers over the years. He learned how important his education really was to his future. He developed a real work ethic. He even developed a sense of humility which is what I attribute the most of his growth to. Larry made a transformation that shows that if you open your mind and allow it to expand, you can transcend the cage you were once locked in.

CHAPTER 27- THE CHURCH REVOLT

They say that when you get your first taste of freedom, you will never be ok with having the shackles on again. To have choice and control of your own life is a beautiful thing. Wake up when you want to, eat what you want, and do what you want are liberating abilities. Whether it be college or just moving out of your parents' house, most people normally get their first taste of this freedom after high school. For me it was going to school. By this time in this story, I had had this freedom for 2 years. I was tenured in freedom or so I thought.

The second week of the season we beat Norfolk State, a team that A&T hadn't beat in 5 years. I recorded 2 huge catches for 50 yards, with one going for a touchdown. The team was hype, and I was feeling like the man. After the game Coach Thomas gave us a great post game speech, which he ended with "We will meet in the stadium parking lot at 8AM to go over to church as a team." This is where he lost me. Going to church in the morning was the last thing on my mind. We had been to church as a team together before. I wasn't the biggest fan of being told it was mandatory for me to get up in the morning after a game and go to church where most likely Coach Thomas would be preaching because he was a deacon. I had enough of him preaching to me during the week.

After the game, I went out with my new quarterback and close friend, Carlton Fears to celebrate the win. Even though I didn't drink anything, we stayed out pretty late. When the sun shone through the blinds the next morning, I was in no hurry to get up. I made an executive decision. I wasn't going. Carlton, who always rode with me, was kind of on the fence. When I told him I wasn't going, he looked like he was contemplating whether to go or not for 20 minutes.

Being the starting quarterback and leader of the team, he said "Man I'm gone go ahead and go." This got me thinking. How is he going to show up and I don't? We were supposed to be in this together. When anyone saw him show up, they saw me. I began to get a little antsy. He was about to walk out the door and walk to the stadium when I said:

"Aight bro, I'm coming."

We drove straight to the church because the team had already left the stadium and pulled up as the last of our team was filing into the church. We hustled inside and grabbed seats in the front row because that was all that was left. The service had the feel of an old-time country Baptist church. A bunch of singing, yelling, and more singing and as I predicted, Coach Thomas was preaching. After church, the coaches spread the word that we would have a team meeting Monday night.

AS THE WORLD TURNS

In this meeting, I sat in my usual seat, front and center. Coach Thomas came in and said something along the lines of we have some guys that don't want to buy into the system. Immediately I knew where this was going. He went on for a second about how guys showed up late to church, some guys complained about having to report to the church, and some guys didn't even show up to church.

Eventually, he called a list of names and you already know my name was on that list. I thought "It is what it is." What pissed me off was after they finished calling the list, I noticed that two people I knew didn't even bother to show up to church were still sitting and hadn't had their names called. If you are going to punish the culprits, get all the culprits. I guess the street code extends to the locker room, because no one ever called out the two guys who got away with the crime. A saying my mother would always say rang in my ears as well. "Don't worry about what anyone else is doing wrong. Make sure you are doing what's right." I could only worry about my actions.

Coach Pope, the new quarterback's coach, led us convicts outside to face our punishment on the hill. Coach Pope had us bear crawling, log rolling, and wheel barreling up and down the hill. We were in the darkness of night and by the time we finished, every last one of us had cursed him out in some form or fashion, while he just laughed and blew his whistle.

As my mind kept rolling around over itself from the log rolls, I decided I was going to just lay in the grass. Trying to focus and prevent myself from throwing up, my mind landed on that ever-daunting question "Is this worth it?"

I contemplated this question for about 3 min as I lay motionless in the dark with my eyes closed. My head was spinning rapidly; it felt like I was still rolling down the hill even though I was still. As the world began to slow its rotation, it was like the answer, after being diluted in the swirling ripples of a lake, began to take shape. The image of me when I was 4 years old wearing a football uniform for Halloween settled behind my eyelids.

I wanted this since the first time I crawled up to a TV, pulled myself up, and glued my eyes on this game. No way this hill, this one moment of frustration and irritation was going to deter me from the thing I felt like I was meant to have. No matter how stupid I thought my situation was at the moment. No matter how many people they brought in to take my place. My mind was worn and beaten but strengthened from being tried. My heart was still magnetized to succeeding in this game.

Without opening my eyes, I took a deep inhale of the grass that my face was using as a pillow. I began to roll up that hill. It was slow and monotonous. I didn't go in a straight line, but I rolled to the top of that hill. I opened my eyes to make sure I had actually made it, and with the world turning over itself again I saw the orange cone we were intended to reach. I tuned everything out, even Coach Pope who was still laughing and carrying on. When I laid in the bed that night with my mind still rolling, I thought "They will not break me."

Looking back on my 20-year-old perspective, there was a flaw. I couldn't see the bigger picture, the unity, spiritual strength, and discipline the coaches were trying to create. I was worried about me and my feelings of freedom. As time goes on, we learn that in order to truly win, it will always be a team effort. A unified effort, spiritually, physically, and mentally. "It's not always about you, but you will always benefit."

CHAPTER 28 - UNBREAKABLE

As the next week began, they continued their punishment of me and those who were late to church. They cut Carlton's reps and made him compete for his starting job. They relegated me to the scout team. The scout team is the group of players normally younger or considered not yet ready to play on Saturdays who gives the starter a look at what the next opponent tends to run. I believe the coaches thought I was going to pout, whine, and feel sorry for myself.

They must have forgotten who they were dealing with. Before I ever got my opportunity to play in a collegiate game, I spent a year on the scout team giving everything I had knowing I wasn't going to play. They didn't know that I spent two years hoping and praying to get in while in high school.

"Your previous challenges are the preparation for your future opportunities."

Going back down to the scout team was like coming back home. My mindset was rebellious but pure. They were not going to break my spirit because they did not understand my past or my "why." I truly wanted to be better than the man in front of me, next to me, behind me, and the man within me. I wanted the respect of my teammates, the men I battled with, not necessarily the coaches. Nothing had changed since I started playing in high school. You can't stop someone whose why is pure and rooted. Ego, accolades, glory, and money can cloud a person's drive toward their goals. When your reason for being in the fight is powerful your mind will "Find A Way" to clear the hurdles in your path.

While on the practice squad, I decided to bring energy and excitement to every play. I wanted to dog the defense, but the underlying goal was to show the younger guys on offense what it looked like to have to earn every day.

The work I had put forth over the past 2 ½ years had catapulted me into a leadership role. I was beginning to see the bigger picture. The nucleus of the future of A&T's offense was supposed to be these guys on the scout team. They needed to feel that what they were doing day in and day out at practice was meaningful. The defense hated us for it and loved us at the same time because we brought it every play. They were accustomed to going through the motions in practice. We let them know early on we were going to score and celebrate if they were chilling.

That's precisely what happened. It happened again and again. Throughout history, variations of the saying "One man can make a difference" has been circulated in society. Most people brush it off as cliché. If we look all around us many of the changes in society were galvanized by the power of a single entity. Then that entity infected the bodies around it toward change. This principle manifested before my very eyes. Everyone on the scout team began to feed off my energy. The mindset was even though the defense knew the play we were about to run, they still won't stop us. The guys who were considered not to be as good or not ready to play were now playing fast. They were playing with energy and enjoying practice. In response our defense turned their temperature up.

Everyone felt it. The players down on the offensive side of the field, the coaches, and the trainers all felt it. I remember after scoring one time I turned back and saw at the offensive starters who were practicing at the other end of the field had paused and were looking at us. I even saw someone down there cheering for us when they were supposed to be focused on their own preparation.

I don't promise you much about life because you have to account for human error, but I will promise this. If you bring a spirit of positivity with you, eventually you will extract the same out of your environment. Energy is one of the most potent transmittable viruses on Earth. Now on the flip side, I can also promise if you carry a stamp of negative energy or pessimism, you can infect the body negatively, like cancer. What environment do you want to create? What environment cultivates winning?

My infectious positive energy was recognized by everyone, including the same coaches who had initially told me after the church incident that I would not dress in our next game against Hampton. Not only did they see what was happening on the field, but they also had to watch it on film every day. There was no escaping it. They reneged and brought me back down to the offense on the third day of practice. I actually think this was the wrong move. This was another instance in which they showed the team that their word was not bond. First, it was Jay and Larry, now it was me.

They brought me down to the offensive side of the field and actually let me get a few reps. This move made the guys who were under the impression they were going to start this week uneasy. That decision built some resentment and anxiety within the ranks. At times it's ok to lose in the here and now to win the championship tomorrow.

The coaches should have sat me, but what they did was weaken the respect from the team. What they did was show that they didn't believe in the other guys to do the job, which helped to diminish their confidence. As I stood behind them chomping at the bit to get in, they felt unnecessary pressure to do something special. They knew I was one play away from being back in the game. While some of our weaknesses were exposed, I believe the coaches did all of this to the team by making a gut reaction looking for a crutch.

My response to them demoting me was the best case scenario. Their reaction to my actions were not. Even though I believe they were wrong from the beginning, I still believed they should have stood strong by sitting me. I was supposed to be standing on the sidelines in street clothes cheering my brothers on. On game day I was dressed and a threat. I was a crutch that reminded the body it was weak.

When the body loses the ability to do something, all the other functions must develop to compensate for the loss. The body will initially be hurt, but if the body or the group continues to work at its deficiencies, the rest of the body will develop well beyond the abilities it previously had. A group or a team is no different. "The loss of, is the opportunity for!" Challenging the body to strengthen itself to overcome a loss, don't increase the overall weakness with dependency of a crutch. Working into the weakness is how a body or a group can become greater than it was before.

They did bring me in the office. They told me because of how I composed myself in the wake of being demoted I had earned my uniform back. They would permit me to dress, but I should not expect to play. I chuckled and thought, "You thought I would shut down because you demoted me. But you don't know why I do this." They still didn't realize nothing they said could hurt me. I was out here for the desire of the game and the love of the men whose eyes I looked in when I ran into the huddle in the third quarter against Hampton.

CHAPTER 29 - INSTANT CLASSIC PART II

It was only one year prior that we ended the longest losing streak in the nation. To beat Norfolk St. this year, who was a perennial power in the MEAC, affirmed the path A&T football was on. Though we felt we were turning the corner, winning is a mindset. A mindset to fight, to overcome an opponent, and even overcoming yourself by "FINDing A WAY". Just as winning is a mindset so is losing. There is a technique to losing. Though we got the taste of winning against Norfolk, Hampton had brought back the mindset that 27 game losing.

The next week we fell deeper into quicksand as we rode up to Myrtle Beach to face Coastal Carolina. We still were not clicking. All the work we had put in and the progress we made seemed to fall apart within two weeks. The grumbles began to get louder throughout the locker room.

As beautiful as a beach can be, our trip to Myrtle Beach was anything but. As if it were an omen, it was windy and gloomy the entire bus ride. The sun never came out for us that day. The game was ugly. At least it was for us. They ran the ball down our throats again and again to the tune of 400 yards on the ground. Our total offense barely eclipsed the 200-yard mark. There was no resilient spirit on our sidelines. Players began yelling at each other. Coaches yelled at players, which turned into coaches yelling at each other. Having all of that happen our fall from our miniscule level of grace was complete.

NEXT PLAY

Just as I lost my first ever football game at Westlake, we had another game the next week. It was a chance to look in the mirror and fix ourselves. Sitting at 2-2 all of our turmoil and strife spiraled right into our biggest rival, North Carolina Central University. This was the first time they had been back to Greensboro since the postgame brawl my true-freshman year. Mutual hate, interestingly enough, can bring opposing forces together. The loathing we had for the buzzards down the highway always brought something different out of us. It brought us back together. As quick as a switch flips the light on, the focus of the team was restored.

This game could not have come at a better time. It was the epitome of the phrase "Next Play," which means let what happened in the past stay there, in the past. Don't dwell on your failures or your successes. Learn from them. The emotion that is attached is no longer valid. We must be as ready as we can for this next moment.

As a team we found the same page and got on it. I was inserted back into my starting role. Carlton, who had been benched in the Coastal Carolina game, was back in his starting spot. We were excited about going into this rivalry. The aura in the locker room and campus seemed to match.

As game day approached, I felt confident. This was not an ill-placed arrogance; it was the feeling that the game plan was perfect. We had watched the film and we knew our opponent. Practices were dynamic and hard-fought. Carlton and I were flowing again. All we talked about in the room was how and where we would beat them. I thought he would get tired of me at some point, but he was down for every second of it.

Walking across campus, random people met us shouting "Beat Central!" The entire campus was vibrating again, "BEAT CENTRAL!" It was on our shoulders to get the pride for an entire nation back. We carried AGGIE PRIDE like a badge of honor into this battle, ready to lay it all on the line for Aggie Nation.

Saturday showed up and the band was rocking, the stands were packed, the tailgate was flooded, and the atmosphere was that of William Wallace from Braveheart preparing to take on the English. At 6 pm the sun was falling, and the scene was set for an epic battle.

We received the ball first. We took the opening drive 72 yards. It was capped off by Carlton hitting me on a seam route. A block from our lone senior receiver Giorgio sprung me into the end zone. "This is going to be easy!"

In the first half, we went on to get two interceptions. They both turned into points adding another touchdown and a field goal. We were ready to take a 17-0 lead into the half. With less than a minute left in the half our defense had them stopped. It was 4th and 12. As they were punting us the ball, one of our rushers senselessly ran into the kicker, drawing a 15-yard personal foul and giving them new life. As if scripted, they hit one of their receivers on the same screen that tormented us two years before for 65 yards. This took them all the way to the 5-yard line. Déjà vu? Or does lightning strike in the same place? They scored in 3 plays with 17 seconds left in the half. The confidence and momentum we built began to shake and it showed in the second half.

Though our defense got a fumble recovery and another interception to start the second half, our offense stalled for an entire 30 minutes of football. While we couldn't crank up the engine, Central clawed their way back into the game to tie us 17-17. As fate had it, we still had a chance with the ball on the 20-yard line to kick a game-winning field goal. Donte Franklin, our freshman kicker, lined up for what we considered a chip shot for him.

Everything seemed so good. Snap, to hold, to ki... As soon as it left his foot, our entire sideline dropped their head. It wasn't even close, landing far left of the goal post. OVERTIME! We wanted to yell and fuss with Donte, but if we wanted him to be ready for another opportunity, we couldn't make him feel any worse than he already felt. We had to refocus to "FIND A WAY" to get this win.

We lost the toss, and they gave us the ball first. In college football both teams get the ball with a chance to score. Whoever has the most points after both teams possess the ball walks away victorious. On our first possession we took the ball down to the 12-yard line but stalled again. Donte trotted back out on the field to redeem himself. Knowing they still had a chance to score after we made our field goal, we weren't as confident as we were 15 minutes before. All eyes on both sides were fixed on Donte. Again, everything looked good from snap, to hold to ki... He missed it again. Their half of the stadium erupted while ours deflated. No one was as empty as Donte. We didn't do a good job of lifting him out of his pit of despair this time either.

The game went on. On their possession our defense held them to a field goal attempt and a chance to take the win. Sadly, for them our defense didn't want to take a chance, so they blocked the kick sending the game into double overtime.

They got the ball first this time and our defense showed up again. We drove them back 10 yards and ended their drive on a loss of downs. "Our turn!" As we trotted onto the field, I wanted the ball. I knew what the game plan was. We attempted to run the ball down their throat again, but they knew we were going to do that. Of course, it didn't work. Frustrated with the decision, I made it known I wanted the ball. I was confident that no one they had could cover me. As the fire within me burned, I stepped out the huddle and glared at the sideline. Not sure if they could feel me or not but the next play came in and I knew I was getting the ball.

"Set Hut" I eyed the safety trying to get him to move as I got into my route. He was patient. He wouldn't budge. I hit the top of my corner route and planted knowing I was going to have to make a spectacular play. Carlton put the ball up before I even got my head around. When I saw it, I gathered myself and elevated. I felt like I was flying above the stadium. I knew I was coming down with this one. Both hands latched on to the ball and I heard the crowd erupt. A feeling of elation bubbled in my gut. As I began my descent back to earth, I felt a strong swipe across my forearms. It was that safety who would not move. I guess he decided to move and come meet me and the ball. My hands began to lose the grip they had on the glory that was assured not even a second before. The ball trickled out of my grasp as I crumpled to the ground and the stadium fell silent.

I sat there for a split second in disbelief. But as fast as that second came, it went away "Next Play." I hopped up and ran back to the huddle. I wanted another chance. I owed Aggie Nation. I owed my teammates. I owed myself the confirmation that I could be as great as I was determined to be.

"I Right 72 Lakers" was the call. I lined up and began scanning the field. After reading the defense I felt I was about to get another chance. Carlton lined up under center. "Set Hut" I attacked the corner covering me. He thought I was going to try to run past him. As he turned to run, I broke across the field on a dig route. He was all turned around. Carlton received pressure so he worked up in the pocket. He saw me as I saw him and let it rip in the middle of the field. As I saw this fastball hurtling toward me, I realized the deep safety was reacting to the ball as well. His reaction was too late as the ball hit my hands and stuck like glue. As soon as I caught it, I turned up field feeling his swipe as I ran past him.

My sights went up field where I saw my brother, Larry, looking for a block to spring me for six. He found one. It just so happened to be the guy that was supposed to be covering me from the beginning. Larry hit him with a bang causing his head to snap back as he fell to the ground. There it was, the goal line into the Promised Land. Our victory was 10 yards away. I burst forward trying to stifle the feeling of excitement that had begun to rise. Suddenly I felt the presence of another defender reaching out to grab me. Instinctively I left my feet and stretched the ball out as far as I could. Picture Michael Jordan in Space Jam reaching out for that final basket with no time left on the clock. When I was a freshman, I wasn't strong enough to carry the defender into the end zone on my first collegiate reception. Through all the work and growth over the last 2 years, today I was strong enough. As he held onto my legs, I continued moving forward. We landed hard on the ground. Looking up to see if I made it, I saw the referee put his hands up to signify "Touchdown Aggies!"

This time the eruption of the crowd lasted and was deafening. Hopping to my feet, amazed by the explosion of the stadium, I looked to my sideline and beckoned the entire team to join me in the end zone. I was too late. Half the sideline was already cleared and heading my way. Coaches, trainers, players, photographers, doctors, administration, cheerleaders, and a few students were swarming the field. My teammates took me to the ground in celebration.

Side note, this was one of the scariest moments of my life because as I was under the pile of bodies I couldn't breathe. When they finally got off me, I was gasping for air. They weren't done. They lifted me on their shoulders and carried me off the field to the stands as we celebrated with the fans.

A moment I will never forget. I reached 100 yards in a game for the first time in my career and recorded two touchdowns. The most important stat of the night was (+1) to the win column.

A transcending feeling of triumph over not only the Eagles of North Carolina Central, but also over the losing mentality we had inherited. In this moment we showed ourselves that we could dig deep within who we already were and be enough. We knew that what it takes is within us. Things will never go as smoothly as planned. We have to adopt a winning belief system. A belief system that says you will achieve. With a winning belief system married with time and effort, winning is on the way.

The scoreboard may not always actually show the win every day, but developing that belief system will prepare you for victory down the line. Effort supported by belief is a potent concoction for success. Are you ready to get into the lab?

CHAPTER 30 - THE AFTERMATH

After the epic victory against Central, we were riding high again. The belief was reignited in the program and into Aggie nation. Our offense had actually clicked. We enjoyed playing for once. Even when the ghost of losses past began to creep upon us, we showed that we could brush it off and stay in the moment. We overcome the moment. That night was amazing on many levels. Amazing what a win can do to you.

We rode high into the next week in a showdown with Morgan State, back to my roots in Baltimore, MD. My family packed out our side of the stands. I was ready but football is a team game. In front of my support system, I almost reached 100 yards again, but we only scored six points on the road, when the other team scored seven. Feeling dejected and defeated we slowly got ready for the disheartening bus ride back to Greensboro. Before we got back on the crowded, stinking, stuffy bus, my family made a play. They embraced me with love and surged me with the power to pick my head back up. They helped me see the good that we did and the things they believed we needed to work on from their honest perspective. The fact that they invested their attention, their intention, and their time impacted me deeply. The fact that they invested a piece of their life into what I was going after, was monumental in building my personal resilience. Love is truly powerful and not to be taken for granted. Cherish those people that cherish you. Be it family or friends, teacher or coach, the love they send to you is more valuable than any dollar you will ever earn. There will be times when you put it all in and still fail. To have a support system there to pick your face out the mud can be lifesaving.

As we hopped back on the bus defeated and dejected, I realized that we were presented with an opportunity to learn a valuable lesson. A lesson Doug Brown had tried to teach me individually as a freshman. Stay humble! Coming off a big win or a big play you have to keep your head. You need to retain all your awareness in the midst of your situation. The slightest loss of focus can result in a dropped ball or a lost game. Focus! A word my father would repeat over and over to me. Where focus reigns, repeated success and growth will follow. When you focus you can see the whole field and attack with that vision.

ALL THE PIECES COME TOGETHER

It's crazy how many ups and downs you can ride, in just one season in your life. The highest of the highs and the lowest of the lows can hit you back to back. I would go on to meet a great coach who would teach us a philosophy that put what Doug and my dad were conveying into poetry. Tom Harper was one year from becoming the force of change we were desperately searching for.

After beating Central we went on a downward slide to finish the season, going 1-4 and ending the year 4-6. Though we improved on a 3-9 season from the year before, we were mountains away from the MEAC championship we set out to be at the beginning of the season.

Though I was able to win receiver of the year again, my success in the classroom was still suffering. I was putting more time in, but I wasn't putting enough in. As an engineering major, the further I progressed in my major the more time my classwork required. At this point, I was still not giving it the attention it deserved. Football was getting all the attention I had between diet, workout, film study, practice, private sessions, and dreaming. I didn't have the energy or time to stay up working practice problems, learning methods, hypotheses, and theorems. We make time for those things that are important to us. So, was it really that I didn't have time? Though essential to my degree, they were not attached to my focus. I had begun to solely focus on Plan A. I did seem to find time and energy for a little something else.

To my standards my all-around performance in 2009 was mediocre at best. I was frustrated with the numbers in the stat book and my grades in the classroom. Though I saw my shortcomings, my coaches saw something in me that they loved. No matter how many quarterbacks played or how bad we were getting beat, I never stopped fighting. I showed up to watch film, put in the work in the weight room, and ran hard in practice as if we were pushing for a championship. They saw I would never give up on my team, even if they benched me.

At the end of spring practice, we had our exit interviews again. I walked from office to office listening to feedback from my receiver coach, offensive coordinator, and lastly Coach Thomas. I began to get the feel that they appreciated what I brought to the team. They saw a lot of potential in me as a playmaker and as a leader. They were building me up instead of the usual tearing down I felt in these interviews. Sitting in front of Coach Thomas, I started to get suspicious as he complimented my performance on and off the field. My skepticism was probably written all over my face. He stopped talking and grabbed a pack of stapled sheets of paper. While grabbing his eyeglasses he began to get to the point.

"Mr. Wallace, we are going to make you whole. Through all your hard work, we have decided to give you a full scholarship." He said in his slow growling voice.

I don't know what happened next. I don't remember saying anything or signing anything to be honest. The next moment I was walking out of the door of the coaches' office zoned out in thought.

A decision to change my cleats by choosing me and who I wanted to be had led me down a path to having the remainder of my education paid for. It was the fighting and dying on the field with Milt. It was the hours of studying plays and studying film. It was the thousands of failures, which set the stage for the thousands of successes that followed. They were all worth it. Everything that had transpired was all worth calling my parents to tell them that we had earned a full scholarship. To hear their excitement blasting through the phone slowed my pace and caused me to really feel where I had come from on this journey. From being mesmerized by Barry Sanders. Standing at the fence with my Aunt Mae. Being the kicker, and watching all my high school teammates signing their scholarship offers on signing day. All of it played a part in molding who I was and who I was becoming. From this moment on my family and I did not have to pay another dime for my undergraduate education.

Keep pushing even when it feels like the progress meter isn't moving much. It may take a thousand failures before you taste success. When you finally taste the sweetness, it will be oh so good. What will be healthier for you is the experience of pushing through failure and struggling through the hard times which will sustain all of the good.

CHAPTER 31 - NEW FOCUS

Determined to be more than what I was after a mediocre redshirt sophomore campaign, I went back to Atlanta for the first part of the summer. I had no internship, no job, and no school. I just focused on turning it up a notch. I felt it was time to transcend past just being happy being on the field and playing. It was time to make a difference.

I worked with Milt. I lifted and ran. I ate properly and rested. I watched film. I made ice baths in my mother's tub. I was introduced to Pilates and tried my first taste of yoga. When Milt wasn't available, I had private lessons with Chad Johnson.

No, I didn't fly to Florida and have in person one on one workouts with one of the greatest route runners that ever lived. I did spend hours watching his drills and his routes on YouTube. I would watch his videos and take notes. When I finished, I would go to the field and train like "Ocho". I didn't drink alcohol. I didn't smoke and I didn't party. Everything I was ever taught about development as an athlete, I put into practice that summer.

I hunkered down in a fort and went to work. I tore apart what I was, to build myself back up stronger than ever. I had six weeks to set a new foundation for myself. It took some time for my body to get accustomed to the load I was putting on it, but I began to feel the changes. The growth in strength and endurance allowed me to do more every time I went into the dungeon.

When it was time to go back to school, I looked different. I felt different. I was different. I was more confident than I had ever been, because I could look in the mirror knowing I put in more work than I had ever put in. I know I said this about the year before, but that's just it. We build on our best to reach new heights. My plan was to leave no doubt who was the number one receiver on the team. The plan was to be the leader in every sense of the word. The plan was to put the entire Mid-Eastern Atlantic Conference on notice. Wallace Miles was here, and the North Carolina A&T Aggies were coming.

I got to campus right before my teammates had scheduled to run a 7 on 7 session. After a 6-hour car ride, I hopped out the car and onto the field without a second thought. I didn't want to miss a rep. To me, it started now with letting everyone know I was all about business this year.

Lewis Kindle, a guy from my high school, was now our new starting quarterback. I knew Lewis in high school as he was our back up in those days. We had a little bit of a connection. He ran a lot of the second team and third team reps in practice. That is where I got most of my opportunities. This was Lewis' second year at A&T, so our connection had a little more time to brew. It was time to serve the entire conference a full serving. Lewis had grown from a 5'9 scrawny limp armed 10th grader into a 6'2 dart thrower. He was creative with his eyes, his throws, and his feet. He had matured into the ideal dual-threat QB who was primed and ready to lead this team.

Lewis and I began to pick up momentum heading into summer camp. We were on the same page on seemingly every play and it showed right out the gate. On the first play of camp, he hit me screeching down the middle of the field on a post route for an 80 yards TD. It was on.

Generally, at the beginning of camp the defense normally shines because they are more reactive and instinctive. The offense is about timing and cohesiveness. When you haven't practiced as an entire unit together for months, there is usually some discontinuity. This year was different. There was nothing they could do to slow us down. Lewis and I were in sync. We could look at each other and see what the other saw. Four seconds later he would meet me somewhere down the field with the ball.

Still not having fully digested my entire serving of that humble pie Doug Brown tried to serve me years before, we celebrated and taunted the defense every play. So much so that eventually the defense put a playful hit out on Jay and I. We demoralized and disrespected the men on the other side of the ball, but they were still our teammates.

One day during another dominating performance by the offense, Lewis called a play in the huddle. Of course, I was confident it would be a completion. I lined down in the slot and looked at the defense. I knew exactly where I was going to get the ball.

At the snap of the ball, I got into my dig route. I knew they were in zone coverage. I took an outside release on the linebacker to give him the impression that I was going vertical knowing he would pass me off to the safety. Once I cleared him, I got my depth. I broke into my dig route, knowing the ball was going to be coming right on the other side of the linebacker I had just cleared. I got my head around quick, but what I saw wasn't the ball coming at me. Lewis was in the pocket trying to elude a few defensive linemen and step up in the pocket. As my first window began to close, with the middle linebacker working to me, I knew there was another hole on the other side of him. I burst over the top of him.

Lewis, feeling what I felt stepped up in the pocket. He whipped one of his patented whistlers at me. Here is where I made a mistake and was taught a valuable lesson. Though I was right to burst into the next hole, you have to remember when you find a hole in a zone, take your time through it. There is something that isn't so nice waiting for you on the other side. I came screaming through the zone, but I felt the edge of the zone closing in on me as fast as I was going through it. In a move for self-preservation, before the ball even touched my hands, I took a peek and saw what my Spidey senses were warning me about. Our weak side linebacker was running right at me. When the ball finally hit my hands, I had lost my focus. My eyes were no longer on the prize. I bobbled it.

When we watched the film, if I had stayed focused on catching the ball, I would have caught it cleanly. I could have gone down with a relatively easy catch. Losing focus for that split second caused me to bobble it. I took one extra step that took me into the collision I was desperately trying to avoid. The linebacker ran through my unprepared body, folding me backward. The hit was hard, but it looked worse than it was. The real issue was that one extra step I took never came out of the ground. As I fell, I felt a pull and then felt a crunching I had never experienced in my life. When I hit the ground, I knew something was wrong. I did not want the defense to get the satisfaction of knowing what I knew. I hopped up quickly as if nothing had happened, but as soon as I went to put weight on my right leg it collapsed.

As I looked down at my leg, a baseball-sized knot was already protruding from my knee. Trying to maintain my composure, I limped my way back to the huddle. The coaches asked me if I was ok. I, of course, said that I was good. When everyone on the field knew I wasn't. I lined up for the next play, but I could barely stand up let alone run the play. I turned around realizing that this was something serious and limped my way over to the training staff.

As much as my mind wanted to get back into practice my body had paid the price of my mental lapse. Anytime a player goes down with a knee injury the first thought is automatically an ACL tear, which requires season ending surgery. See how we are automatically trained to think the negative thoughts. We have to learn to see incidents for what they are and take our negative anxieties out of it.

We later found out that I had suffered a severe sprain to my MCL. The prognosis was a 4-6-week recovery. The first game was exactly four weeks away. A shade of darkness began to cloud my head with negative thoughts. My knee was so badly swollen and sore I had to drive home with my right leg swung over in the passenger seat, while I hit the pedals with my left. "How am I going to be ready for the season when I can't even walk?"

All it takes is a split second of lost focus. Whether you're driving down the street, at work, in a relationship, or running across the middle of the field on a dig route, a loss of focus can end in disaster. After all the preparation you put in, all it takes is a split second for the plan you envisioned to be erased and leave you with a blank canvas. Sometimes it's a minor setback or it may put you out of commission. A loss of focus can be lethal.

Before getting on the road to school, going into a game or even going out at night, "FOCUS!" Whatever you decide to do in this world and wherever that path takes you, always remember your focus. It will allow you to maintain your awareness at every peak and valley of the journey. You have heard the saying, "success lies in the details." Focus will enable you to see the details, retain the details, execute the details, and ultimately find that success. "FOCUS!"

CHAPTER 32 - A PHONE CALL CAN CHANGE YOUR LIFE

Brinnnnnnng…Brinnnnnng…

"Hey lady, how are you doing?"

"Ummmm, I'm ok.

"What's Up.?

"I gotta tell you something."

"What's up?"

"I'm pregnant!"

A long, seemingly endless pause followed that statement. My heart started racing. My entire future flashed before my eyes. Thoughts like having a kid, dropping out of school, getting a job, and traveling to see my child flooded my mind. I had no intentions of having a relationship with the young lady I had chosen to lay down with, but I had every intention of being a good father, sending child support every month, and fighting for custody. Imagining watching my child grow up from a distance, weighted my heart down. Thinking about what it was going to take to overcome not being present in my child's life on a day to day basis, killed my spirit. I got caught with my nose wide open and my head, not on a swivel. That escalated quickly right.

Let's rewind this picture two years. My focus was on football. I ate, slept, and drank football. I was still a man, a young man at that. My first year away from home, I didn't have the boundless sexual experiences that they say you are going to have when you get out on your own. That year my girls were football, Calculus, and Biology. That year was pretty bone dry if I can be honest. That might have been ok if everywhere I turned, my peers weren't recounting these stories of their late night, mid-day, and early morning escapades. They spoke of this girl, that girl, and these girls. I felt like I was the only one who was not having the full college experience. There was my first flawed thought process. When you grow up in a world where the guys who have sex with a lot of girls are celebrated, more girls want him, and other guys respect him, it's easy to inherit those ideals through osmosis. Being engulfed with this ideology took a life of its own in me. We grow up in the home, but we are raised in the totality of our environment. We spend more of our time awake outside in the world. This corrosive thinking gets instilled in young men from a young age.

Way back in elementary school we played a game called "I'm in the game." The whole goal was to grab as many girls' butts and breast as possible throughout the day and say, "I'm in the game"! The crazy thing is as a boy you had to be invited into the game by a girl. This is a societal issue. Sexuality is not taught correctly; it's barely taught at all. Yea we learned what a vagina and a penis are in health class, but there are emotional, psychological, and sociological pieces to two people agreeing to give themselves to each other. Consent is a lecture in itself.

It is perfectly fine to indulge in protected sex with a consenting person of age, who is aware of the ramifications that sex may bring. If you connect with someone and that connection takes you to the bedroom with mutual respect for the actions taking place, by all means, connect. You may find one. You may end up with hundreds, I'm not going to shame you either way. As long as you are not scheming, using, or degrading the other person and they understand the nature of the relationship, by all means protect yourselves with a condom and enjoy.

Let's get a little gritty. As fun and exciting as sex is, always remember, sex is an adult act, with adult repercussions. There are some forever things that can come from not protecting yourself. It's no secret. STD's are real and can affect your life forever. A baby is real, and will affect your life forever. You are going to hear this over and over and over. It may get to the point that you feel it's cliche, but trust me, just because it's cliche does not make it any less real.

Problems arise when you have the thought process of the sophomore version of me. I assumed everyone I knew was getting it in and I was dried out on a desert. I made a decision on my way back to school my sophomore year.

Now before I let this out the bag, I sincerely apologize to any woman I courted that year and the subsequent years to follow. I apologize for the naivety and ignorance I acted upon. There was a song that was out in Atlanta at the time that had an exciting beat and a very profane chorus. The song was entitled "Wassup Wit Dat Cookie." I decided this was going to be my motto.

Sometimes you look back at who you were in the past and all you can do is shake your head in disbelief that you could be so ignorant. In the next moment you have to be thankful for growth because you could still be stuck in whatever place that was.

All my life I had been given the label "the nice guy." The nice guy doesn't get a plethora of girls and gets joked on by the guys for not getting any girls. I was tired of both of these and I decided that I was going to change the personal narrative of my relational life. It was going to come at the expense of my integrity and the respect of the women I encountered. These thoughts are what got me in the predicament that I found myself in going into my fourth year of school. I had gotten a young woman pregnant. A woman whom I had no feelings for. A woman I had coerced to open herself up to my childish goals.

As an athlete there are four things to do in summer school: your sport, school, working and hanging. When you're done with your sport activities, classes are over, and if you don't have a job all there is left to do is hang out. Hanging encompasses a multitude of activities, many of which are not very sanctified. My drug of choice was sex.

Where my first year was a barren desert, year two, the seas began to open up. When I realized what I was doing, I loved the feelings sex produced. The feeling of dominance, the feeling of being so close you can feel the physical and emotional affects you can have on another person. The mental freedom it induces. The competition between the two involved and of course the journey culminating in the climax.

"Well, what had happened was," I was on this journey with a young lady and while using protection, it broke. Of course it did! My pull-out game was still in its infantile stages. Boom! Pregnant! It doesn't take much. Now what?

"I'm about to be a father" cycled through my head constantly as I went through my days. I was going to become a statistic, perpetuating the stereotype of the young black man fathering children before marriage. I was thinking about how much my life was about to change. My childish goals allowed me to lay down with a woman whom I did not have intentions of marrying. In no way am I saying she was a bad person. Being honest with myself, I knew the only reason I ever spoke to her was for what happened in that bedroom. We hear about the consequences of laying down with someone such as pregnancy or STD. When they hit your life, most people are stunned like it's a shock. I wonder why that is? "They told us!"

I received this news one week after my knee injury. What seemed to be setting up to be my best year, was now totaled before we had even pulled off the lot. I didn't tell anyone initially. I was afraid of the judgment that would be passed on me. Even though this was something that frequently occurs in our society, it wasn't supposed to happen to me. What I learned later on is we don't have to blast our issues to the public but, we sure as heck better own them.

CHAPTER 33 - WHEN IT RAINS...

As I sat out, Aggie football didn't stop for a moment. Practices and meetings rolled on as if I had never been there. Knowing you are just a car in the assembly of the train was a pretty humbling feeling. Day in and day out I had to watch my teammates do what I had grown to love while being restricted to spectating.

I was beginning to feel as if I was losing my ground. I didn't care if I had to walk around with crutches or drive with my left foot. It didn't matter that I could only sleep 15 minutes at a time because the second I moved the excruciating pain woke me up. These things I knew would pass. What I could not accept was I was losing the time on the field to get better and be with my teammates. Football is unforgiving. Someone could rise and replace me just like that. To sit and watch them was demoralizing. It was also invigorating.

I hated being where I was, so the only option in my mind was to do everything in my power to get healthy as fast as I could. I made sure I was at every opportunity for rehab. I was gifted with one of our physical trainers, Mallori, to guide me through this challenge. I came to see her every day. No matter how sore or depressed I was, I limped into the training room. I did whatever she instructed, no matter how much it hurt. No matter how much I would complain amid the pain, I wanted more. The great thing about Mallori was that she didn't care about all the whining I was doing. It was like she was more in tune with my body and what it was capable of than I was. She was constantly laughing at me as she challenged my strength and range of motion.

Recognize real riders, even if they have to beat you down to build you up. Some people will show you the good that humanity is capable of. Mallori was one of those people who ran up in my life ready to ride!

...IT POURS

One week before the first game of the season, we held an inter squad scrimmage. A tune-up before the real thing. Either the offense had regressed, or the defense had caught up and surpassed us. Whatever it was we were struggling. The defense was making all kinds of plays and making all kinds of noise.

Toward the end of the scrimmage, Lewis dropped back for a quick pass. What he didn't realize was one of our big defensive linemen, Micah Stanfield, also dropped back into zone coverage. Not seeing Micah, Lewis threw the ball right at him. For a big man, Micah was surprisingly agile.

Micah jumped up and intercepted the ball. Looking like a small J.J. Watt, Micah gathered his feet and began rumbling down the sideline. This was the exclamation point on the dominating performance by the defense but something else was brewing. Everyone on the field had stopped chasing him and watched as he celebrated toward the end zone. Everyone except Lewis, who had taken an angle to catch Micah before he reached the end zone. When Micah realized Lewis was coming, he prepared to fight him off. Lewis, instead of colliding with him, jumped on his back.

You would have expected Lewis to wrestle Micah to the ground or Micah to stiff arm the quarterback and walk into the end zone. The rare option C occurred. Instead of pulling Micah to the ground, Lewis crumbled to the ground, grabbing his knee.

When your starting quarterback is on the ground holding his knee, the breath of the entire program is sucked out. Every person on the field fell silent. The entire field froze. The only people moving and probably the only people breathing were Micah, who was celebrating in the end zone, not realizing what happened, and the training staff who was running toward Lewis.

Most successful football teams rely on a skilled quarterback to be a great player and a great leader. Those qualities are often hard to find together in one person. We had been blessed to have found Lewis, who exhibited both of these qualities on the football field. Writhing on the ground, it immediately put the success of our entire season on red alert. It put some of our coaches' livelihoods in jeopardy and put players' dreams in harm's way. Though we had other people to fill the position of quarterback, as I stated before, it's rare to have the combination of qualities Lewis possessed.

As he hobbled off the field, the rumors began to swirl. "Baby Lew may be out for the season." I didn't want to believe it. Not now, not when we had finally felt our passing game was ready to be a major contributor to the success of the team. Escorted by the training staff, Lewis walked off the field frustrated. Seeming to symbolize the success of our season walking out on us.

The MRI did prove Lewis had torn his ACL and was done for the season. When I went to see him in the hospital after his surgery, I went in wanting to make him feel better and feel supported. In fact, he made me feel better about the situation. I could tell he was frustrated but he was pretty calm and receptive of what was going on. He understood the journey that was before him, but he seemed ready to tackle the challenge. It was a somber but uplifting moment.

Going into what was supposed to be my breakout year, I was injured. I had a baby on the way and my quarterback, the guy that gave us the best opportunity to win was now gone for the entire year.

The mental stress started to show itself. Fear and stress are always in your mind. They can be psychologically paralyzing. A mental ball and chain created from the perception of what could happen. Many times, it has nothing to do with what really "is." These fictitious creatures can stop the strongest of us in our tracks because our beliefs fall to their shadows. In our moments where fear and stress begin to grab hold of our minds, we must remind ourselves that the thing we think can happen hasn't happened. There is still a possibility for the outcome we desired or an even greater result. My career didn't have to be in jeopardy. Having a child didn't have to deter me from my dreams. The next quarterback may flourish with this new opportunity.

It applies to all areas in life. I will shine in this interview and will get the job. Getting fired is the kick in the ass I needed to pursue my purpose. These types of thoughts can have the same chance of happening, as does the negative to each of them. We tend to want to swim to the bottom of the deep end of the emotional pool. Fear and stress are self-imposed obstacles that we must overcome before we approach the real challenge. F.E.A.R is False

Evidence Appearing Real. You have the power to dissolve it without lifting a finger.

When we feel stressed, overwhelmed or even afraid our bodies also go through chemical processes. Defense mechanisms engage to help us prepare for the supposed threat. We tense up and we lose our focus. My body decided to show the world what I was feeling internally. On top of everything that I perceived to be negative, I began to develop a stress related skin rash.

Envision skin disorders such as psoriasis or eczema. I had allowed my mind, the one thing I should have control of in this world at all times, to begin to affect my body adversely. It started as one spot. By the time it ran its course, it covered most of my torso, arms, legs, and neck. I felt like a leper. I was afraid to take my shirt off in front of people and my confidence plummeted. I wore turtlenecks and hoodies in the summer. It constantly itched. My only relief was a lukewarm shower.

Now injured, baby on the way, quarterback out for the year, and a leper. I felt I had hit rock bottom. One month before I was approaching the summit of my mountain. Now I felt downtrodden and broken.

There is so much power in the mind to combat the destructive forces inside and out. When it seems everything is going wrong, the starting place to counteract the adversity seemingly being imposed upon you, is to fortify your mind and your thoughts, utilize *The Secret*. Fertilize and feed your mind. Sometimes "when it rains, it pours." Are you going to drown in the sorrow or are you going to realize that everything that grows needs water?

CHAPTER 34 - COMEBACKS AREN'T ALWAYS FAIRYTALES

Headed into the first week of the season, the stage was set. In front of us was one of our in-state rivals, Winston Salem State, again. My rehab was coming along, but I was not ready to play. I had gotten back to running straight ahead and graduated to cutting. This was the final hurdle before returning to the field. Every day I walked into rehab, I thanked Mallori for all she was doing. As I walked out, I was back to fussing at her while she returned a malevolent smirk.

I was apprehensive when we started working on change of direction because it felt like my knee was going to give out. I had no faith that this thing was going to hold up, but Mallori stayed in my ear, "Trust it."

As the week continued, I began to push it more and more. I trusted Mallori and was beginning to trust that the work we had put in to strengthen my knee was good enough. I was feeling better, and it showed more and more. Every day I was sore and in pain after, but every day was better than the next.

When game day arrived, I was about 75 percent of my full potential. They dressed me for the game, but told me there was very little chance that I was going to play. I was only there for an utter and complete emergency. The emergency never came that night, but the first loss of the season did. We looked out of sync on offense. This loss further increased the spread of the fear of where our season was headed with Lewis down for the year.

THE BABY

Being an immature and at times selfish young man, I only cared about how I felt. I cared about what I wanted. My selfishness, lack of empathy, and lack of love created tension between the soon to be mother of my child and me. It felt like she began to do things to spite me. She would tell me what day the doctor appointments were, but it seemed like she would always disappear on the day of. I didn't know where to show up. Then she would text or call me that night with the results from the doctor. After the third time it began to really anger me, but she was not the root of my anger. My anger was multifaceted, but the rage I had developed for the world was focused on her.

Week 2 I finally made it back on the field, but we were still lost. My skin condition was steadily spreading, and I wasn't 100% healthy. All kinds of thoughts were flowing through my head and the anger began bubbling up within me and I did not know how to harness the energy. It began to spill out all over the place. I even went as far as defaming the character of the soon to be mother of my child, by establishing doubts that the pregnancy was even real in the first place. This only increased the tensions between us.

The dagger that pierced my heart was another day when I was supposed to be told when and where the doctor's appointment was supposed to take place. Sitting in my *Circuits II* class, I received a text message containing an image. There it was with my name in the top left corner. The image was of my newly forming son! A whirlwind of emotions began swirling. I didn't know how I was supposed to feel, but I was going to be the father of a baby boy.

That's what every man wants. I was angry that she did not allow me to be a part of this amazing moment. I was confused about what to do and nervous because this lifelong burden was real. I put my phone away and I tried to refocus for the remainder of the class, which was nearly impossible. Though I sat, eyes glued to the board. I was lost in plain sight.

THIS IS JUST WHAT IT IS

I made it back from injury, but with Lewis out, we played with four different quarterbacks throughout the year. We even pulled a baseball player off the baseball team in the middle of the season. We were unable to build any cohesiveness with any of them before the next quarterback was thrown in. We started the season off 0-4, last in the conference and last in the nation, again. Besides the ray of sun that found its way through my window every morning, there wasn't much shining in Greensboro, NC.

All the hard work, all the confidence, and the prophecy was gone. The rash had spread over my entire body constantly flaring up. Even with all the negativity whirling around me I didn't stop working. I trusted Mallori. I trusted the process. I trusted the vision that projected inside of me. Though nothing seemed to be going my way, all I knew was if you stop, you won't. If you stop, you don't even give yourself a chance to come out on the other side.

In the movie "Notorious", P. Diddy's character played by Derek Luke, famously says "You can throw me butt-naked in the jungle and I'll come out with a chinchilla coat, a leopard hat, and 10 pounds heavier from eating them." What does that person really look like walking out of the jungle? You might imagine him walking out with an angelic light shining behind him. His walk hitting every beat of "Juicy" playing in the background and a fresh chinchilla draped over his shoulders. "That's cute!" But what's realistic is he is scarred from head to toe from the battles with those forces that wanted to eat him. Feet cracking from the treacherous terrain of the winding maze. Blood mixed with sweat dripping from his face, as he walks to his own beat. Leopard skin draped over his shoulders still bloody from the violent death it had to suffer. That's the warrior that would emerge from the jungle. Stronger, more resilient, and empowered over his own mind. That's the image we must become. This life thing isn't always pretty like the movies.

There will come a day. It may be today that you will find yourself in your own struggle, in your own jungle, and in a test of how hungry you are. Keep pushing and keep moving toward what you feel is yours. Even if you come to a dead end and feel like you've wasted your time, you haven't. The experiences gained on your way have prepared you for the journey back and the journey forward. Those steps are just part of your life's journey. They are essential to the success of your story.

CHAPTER 35 - FEEL THE SUN

The weight I was carrying began to get too heavy. I broke down and opened up to my parents about the pregnancy. A conversation I had been dreading for months. They both responded differently than I expected. Neither was mad or irate, but calmly disappointed. Neither panicked, which relieved some of the tension within me. One thing I have learned from my parents over the years about perceived negative situations is to breathe in deep and say "Ok, what's next!" It's a way to absorb whatever the circumstances are at the time and begin moving forward. At this time, I had not yet mastered the technique. Their demeanor covered me in comfort that we were going to make this work.

While the realization that I was about to become a father was becoming more and more real, the way the season was going was unreal. Game after game, quarterback after quarterback turned into loss after loss. The coaches had lost me the year before after the church incident, but now it seemed they had lost the entire team. The enthusiasm built from the end of the summer was gone. Players and even coaches seemed at times to be going through the motions. As a leader of the team, I was lost for words. What do you say to a team that has fought, put it all on the line, tried its best to execute and their efforts lead to defeat, every week? Really, what do you say that will make a difference in the moment?

As in all storms, the sun will shine through, even if just for a moment. Sitting at 0-7, the one bright spot of the season came one abnormally sunny day in mid-October when the Bison of Howard University came to town. On this day, the clouds parted, the rains stopped, and my rash had finally shown signs of clearing up. The feeling the team had been missing returned if only for a moment.

Having my two youngest nephews in the stands watching me play for the first time, gave me the inspiration I was in dire need of. Their presence brought a smile to my face and a fire to my heart. We played with passion and fun on both sides of the ball. The offense had two 100 yard receivers. This had not happened in years. Our running back Mike Mayhew went over 100 yards and had two scores. I matched him with two scores. The defense recorded two interceptions and a fumble recovery that they returned for a touchdown. By the end of the day, we walked off the field with a 52-32 victory, the most points I had seen an A&T team put on the scoreboard. Though this didn't catapult us on a winning streak, or win us a championship, it was good that we could feel this feeling again. It reminded us why we strapped it up every day. This reminded me of when I was a senior in high school and our soccer team went 0-10. Seeing us score had so much more significance than if we were always winning. Seeing us win and celebrate even in the midst of a terrible season showed us that the feeling was still there, we just needed to dig even deeper to hold on to it.

When you are going through those rough times in life, catching a glimpse or getting a brief taste of success will help that mental battle of staying in the fight. Even if it's a minor victory, cherish it like it's fertilizer to your future success. Allow it to be the plant food keeping the seed of your dreams and ambitions alive. Feeling the joy of what you are fighting for, even if it is for a brief moment, can reinvigorate the feelings of why you started in the first place. All momentum has to have a starting place. A powder keg in a dark place is harmless, but all it takes is a tiny spark for it to explode.

This win was a reminder to us of the type of team we could be. We lost the remaining two games that season finishing an abysmal 1-10 record. I believe the memory of that win against Howard helped propel us into what the future was about to bring. One thing I will always remember Coach Thomas say was "A minor setback is a setup for a major comeback!" 2010 was easily my worst year as an

Aggie, but what comes after the darkest night when you stay in the fight? The opportunity of a new day.

CHAPTER 36 - ANOTHER LOSS

After all those L's I took in 2010 I couldn't bear any more. At least I didn't think I could.

"Hello"

"Hey, how are you doing?"

"I have to tell you something!" She said,

"What's up?" I responded confused.

With a soft but clear voice, she said: "There is no more baby."

These words left me stunned and frozen, again. I had just begun to get excited about the possibility of being a father. I had completely accepted that this woman was going to be my child's mother. As much as the news of the pregnancy had scared me, this news sucked all I had left out of me. We were too far along for an abortion, so I couldn't imagine what happened. Eventually, I gained enough stability to ask, "What do you mean? What happened?"

She told me that while she was back home over winter break in Massachusetts, she was walking down some stairs in the snow she slipped on some ice and fell. She said they rushed her to the hospital where the doctor gave her the grim news that she had lost the baby.

Enraged, my first thought was, "You idiot! What the hell? Why weren't you more careful?" That was an emotional response built from the rollercoaster I had been on for months. Luckily, I resisted blurting out my first thought. The next vision that flooded my mind were the images of my son and I. The being I was going to be entrusted with dissolving away to nothingness. Next, I thought about the turmoil that she must have been going through. This news was traumatic to me, but I only heard about it. She lived it. She experienced it. She will never unsee it. She will never unfeel it. So, what came out of my mouth was a calm and sincerely empathetic "Are you ok?"

Inside I was writhing with confusion! "Does this happen in real life?" "How could this happen to us?" I was angry that she wasn't more careful. I felt sorrow that life was lost, the life of my son. There was empathy for all she had to go through — the pain of the incident and the abortion that followed to remove our lifeless son from her womb. What could she be going through mentally?

I would not be being honest with you if I told you there wasn't another feeling also swirling in the pot. As traumatic as the journey to this point was, I felt an eerie sense of relief because as much as I had trained myself to want this future, I honestly didn't want it. I took the class and failed the test. This experience is what drove in the lesson. When you lay down with someone, you have to be ready for the possible effects that comes with that decision. I know you may have read that thinking I'm cool we will use a condom, or your strong pull-out game will save you. That's fine. Life is the most real teacher there ever will be. If you don't listen now, life will show you in its own twisted way.

I was set free but I felt emotionally broken down. The only thing I knew to do was take a deep breath and think "What's next?". Go to the gym and get on the field. Go to study hall. Go to study groups. Hang out with friends. Though I put on a mask to conceal the pain I was feeling, this mask helped me step back towards the path. When we go through pain, we must deal with it at some point. Mental and emotional trauma is like surviving a gunshot wound with the bullet still lodged in your leg. If we don't dig into the pain, to extract the source, the bullet, we will never regain our full stride. The pain will always be there under the surface holding you back in some piece of your life. If it's counseling, confiding in a mentor, a close friend, or a parent somehow, someway, we have to get the bullet out!

FOURTH QUARTER

"PUT THEM FOURS UP"

CHAPTER 37 - NEW BEGINNINGS

Prior to returning to school from winter break, I was met with more news that would cause another huge change in my life. My head coach Howard Thomas and his entire staff had been fired. "Here we go again!" I am going to have to impress yet another coaching staff and earn what I have already earned twice before. Remember, again, your previous experiences prepare you for your future challenges/opportunities.

With this change, I had thoughts of transferring to another school. I was tired of losing. After the previous season, I was searching for a way out of that environment. I was adamant about finding a place to play that had a winning culture. I checked out coaching staff tenures and quarterback statistics. I checked their receivers' stats and body types. I watched film on teams to see what type of offense they ran, even making sure the school offered my major. I was committed to transferring and finding the right situation for me to be successful. What I was really trying to do was run from the pain and find an easy solution in my recovery. During my time being hurt, a seed was planted. Rehabbing into the pain was the most powerful way to recover.

During my investigation period, A&T signed a new head coach, Tom Harper. Coach Harper was coming from Jackson State University where he had won a SWAC Championship and finished in the top 2 in his division all 4 years as the head man at Jackson. Coach Harper had played at North Dakota and spent time as an assistant coach at the University of Missouri, Boston College, Georgetown, and his alma mater. He got his first head coaching opportunity at our rival Winston Salem State University where he won two CIAA championships in 5 years. No doubt about it, he was a winner. He took programs that were mediocre to conference champions and Black College National Champions. His resume piqued my interest, so I decided to see what the spring would bring.

Coach Harper set the tone from our first team meeting. He said what I thought was the worst opening line to a new team you could ever say, "As we stand now this team is not very good!"

Immediately tension sprouted throughout the entire room. Who is this guy to come in here, not knowing any of us from a loaf of bread? He did not know what we had gone through to tell us that we weren't very good. He did not know how much talent was in this room. He must not have known that we went into battle every week with half the scholarships of every team we lined up against.

I later learned that he did know. He knew every ounce of the circumstances that he decided to enter into. What I learned was that he looked at situations objectively. Take the emotion out of it and see it for what it is so you can proceed from the real place you are. We were a 1-10 team. Obviously not very good, but I was caught up in my emotions. After that first meeting I got back on my search for an escape route.

Coach Harper made everyone uncomfortable. It was part of his genius. No one or any position was safe. You knew it from the first day of spring conditioning. In my first four years we did these spring workouts called "mat drills" in the school's auxiliary gym. It was uncomfortable but we were in a conditioned space. This new administration took us outside in the middle of winter where we were at the mercy of the elements. Temperatures in the mid 30's at 6 AM wearing nothing but sweat suits that seemed to never be warm enough. Rolling, running, changing direction, up downs, sprints, and bear crawling on the thawing morning dew. Four years in and Coach Harper had me back to square one. He had me checking in to see if my heart and my mind were still in this. "Do I really want to put myself through this again? How bad do you want this? How hungry are you? My answer was simply, "Chinchilla!"

It's tough to catch your breath when you're tired and the cold air is pulling the air from your lungs. It's tough to keep moving when you're soaking wet from sweat and dew in the freezing cold. It's tough waking up at 5 am knowing what you are intentionally about to put yourself through. Tough is temporary. Your muscles will adapt to anything you challenge them to do consistently. Remember, your brain is a muscle too. Every day we challenged ourselves to adjust to the strain. Over the course of 6 weeks, our bodies and minds were consistently challenged. Our minds and bodies reacted by adapting to the increased load allowing for a greater capacity.

CHAPTER 38 - WHO TRY'N TO BOX

We thought when we finally put on pads as spring came around things would slow down. We thought we could just get back to playing ball. We were sorely mistaken. Just like anything being renovated you have to tear pieces down to build it back up stronger. The pressure Coach Harper and his staff put on us at times wore down our mental states. So much so that we began to turn on each other. Fights were a normal occurrence in spring ball and summer camp, but that all changed this year. The first fight set the precedence. These coaches had a peculiar way of handling them.

They stopped practice and had the entire team surround the two combatants. One pair of boxing gloves appeared out of nowhere. Both fighters put one glove on, while putting the other hand behind their back. "Ding", it was on. We witnessed a bunch of wild flailing, a few solid connections, but a winner could not really be determined. What did happen was, both fighters got completely exhausted and at the sound of the coach's whistle, the fight was over. In all the excitement we didn't realize what was coming next. Another whistle sounded and Coach Harper yelled "Start it over!" "Start what over?" I thought. "The Fight?" No, he meant to start practice over from the beginning. The coaches herded us back to our warmup lines and made sure that the two that were just fighting were in front.

For some odd reason, we didn't have another fight that spring. The lesson within the madness was that losing our cool in the midst of battle did not make us better men or a better team. It did nothing but waste a bunch of energy, cause us to lose our focus, and then set us back. Fighting in a game is a 15 yard penalty, for the team!

Every change comes with adjustments and with those adjustments comes growth. It can also cause decay. The choice is always in your hands. We had players that thought they were bigger than the program. Just like with Coach Thomas, Coach Harper wasted no time in removing guys with that mentality from the team. I had a brief bout of complaining about the new regime, and even I was put on notice, quickly. Though I was still looking to transfer out, I couldn't mess up the boat keeping me afloat. I got my act together. One moment of rebellion is not worth throwing away the years of preparation you have put in to get to the place you've reached.

You must have your own personal goals. But must understand this, you need the system to prevail. No man has ever truly done anything worthwhile alone. Someone taught the basics, someone supported, someone encouraged, and someone got you the ball. This applies to your life's dreams and how many touchdowns you score. Be in the moment, but think bigger than how you feel in the moment. Never allow your ego, selfishness, or pride to cause you to think you are bigger than the program. It may not function the same as if you were there, but it will keep moving. It will find another you. What people will really hold to when all these individual moments are gone, is your legacy. Don't let your ego, selfishness, and pride cut your legacy short. Are you trying to box, or do you want to build a legacy that lives on long after you have moved on?

CHAPTER 39 - I SEE YOU CAM

Friday, April 28, 2011, I was sitting in Bluford Library intending to pull an all nighter in preparation for an exam. I was more tuned in to what was happening in New York City, than I was in the book six inches from my face. I was watching a live stream broadcast when I heard Roger Goodell, Commissioner of the Nation Football League, utter words that I will never forget: "With the first pick in the 2011 NFL Draft the Carolina Panthers select, Cam Newton from the University of California."

In my eyes, since the beginning of my football career, I had been told I wasn't a football player. Though I had overcome the detractors' opinions, subconsciously I always had a sense of doubt that maybe I was only supposed to go so far. Hearing and seeing this monumental moment affected me tremendously. For the first time in my career, I truly believed there was a place beyond where I thought the finish line was. Even though I felt the key turn in the meeting with Rags, my freshman year, it never really turned over and got in gear until this moment. As I watched my high school quarterback walk across that stage, shake the commissioner's hand, and don the Reebok embroidered Chargers hat, it clicked in my head "I can do this. I'm going to do this." The end of my college career was now a checkpoint, a comma, not a period. I had shared the field with a real-life person. He had taken his abilities beyond high school, beyond college, and into the dream of millions of young men. He was going to make a life out of this game we loved.

Watching Cam throughout the draft process, I felt myself in the places I saw him. The day after seeing him at the NFL Combine in Indianapolis, IN, surging with energy, I stood up in the middle of our stretch lines and yelled "365 DAYS UNTIL THE COMBINE!" For the rest of the spring, every day we did anything football related, I yelled out the countdown. I wanted to speak that energy into everything I did. I wanted my teammates to hear me and hold me accountable. I wanted them to feel that energy and strive to work with me on the journey. Mostly, I wanted to remind myself everyday what I was working toward.

"Curtis Walls to workout with the St. Louis Rams."

"Nick Clement, Free Safety NC A&T, makes his debut with the Toronto Argonauts".

"Donte Poole signs with the Cleveland Browns."

As I saw these headlines it made the idea of me playing professional football more tangible. I had shared the field with these men, competed with these men, and trained with these men. In my mind I had been on the same level as these men and could be on the same level with these men. I could see, smell, taste, and hear this idea. All that was left was to grasp it.

When I arrived back home for my final offseason, my dad asked me what I wanted to do after graduation. I told him:

"Dad, when I saw Cam walk across that stage, something hit me. I remember being in the same building and on the same field as the best player in the entire country. It made me realize that NFL players aren't preordained mythical gladiators. I'm going to play professional football. Seeing Cam made that real to me."

"OK, but don't forget you will have an Electrical Engineering degree." My mother who was in ear shot said.

I didn't say anything, but I thought of something I had heard Will Smith say "There is no reason to have a Plan B because it distracts from Plan A." I was "ALL IN!

We have heroes that we admire from afar. They normally epitomize something great. They display abilities, attributes or hold positions we fantasize about. The separation between us and that person normally creates a heroic factor that makes them seem almost godly. It can seem that they are just different and meant to be where they are. The possibilities of you getting to that place seem farfetched.

Even though we are all connected by six degrees of separation, it is something about having a direct connection with someone who reached where you dream to be. Makes your goal seem that much more realistic to your life. That connection may come in the form of a big brother, a classmate, or a training partner. Maybe it's a high school teammate whom you hadn't seen in 4 years, walking across the NFL Draft stage, and shaking the commissioner's hand. A smile brightened by the resilience, the work, and the passion that it took to get to that place. He also represents the place you both were at one point in life's journey. He represents a piece of you reaching that place. The question you will have to ask yourself is are you ready to take the rest of you there?

If so, be conscious that as you move toward your place you will become the Cam for someone you meet along your journey. Carry yourself like you will inspire someone that needs a Cam in their Life. See the Cam, to make it real for you. Then be the Cam, for the next you!

CHAPTER 40 - WORK IS NOT ALWAYS FUN AND GAMES

I came home in May of 2011 mentally ready to attack my last off-season. All I could think about was how hard I was about to train to get ready. But before my training got to rolling my father abruptly confronted me with this statement: "You need to get a job!" For someone who was focused on getting ready for football and graduating, a job was the furthest thing from my mind. I understood what he was trying to do for me, but that didn't mean I was all for it.

As if they had been scheming on me, my mother turned around and said "Your Uncle Wayde, might be looking to hire someone in his warehouse. He manages and operates a distribution warehouse."

Upon their command I called Uncle Wayde who is really my mother's first cousin, but he was there for me like an uncle my entire life. Uncle Wayde quickly set up an interview with me. Thinking nepotism was in play, I was sure I was going to get the job. I came in a bit lax for the circumstances. Uncle Wayde changed the atmosphere with the seriousness and professionalism of his tone, posture, and approach. He treated this interview as if I were anyone else and I understood. Though we were family, his decision to hire me would affect his productivity, his job, and livelihood. The success or failure of his employees directly affected his production and the lifestyle he had developed for himself. Family or not this was a serious situation.

He did go on to hire me, but I grew to appreciate his approach. He showed me what professionalism looked like. He was down to do whatever it took to get the job done correctly. I gained a lot of respect for him as a leader. I saw him 25 feet in the air sweating in a wife-beater, with slacks and dress shoes on pulling orders. Staff was low or orders were high one day. He usually did his work from a cozy air-conditioned office with a crispy straight from the cleaners white dress shirt on. This day he showed us he was down for the cause.

Let's paint the picture. There were about 16 aisles. Each aisle was about 150 feet long and 30 feet high. I had to get over my slight fear of heights quickly. At the time, I was required at times to be 25 feet in the air picking and counting individual items to fill the order on the packing slips. My job was to walk around the airplane hangar sized warehouse and pick items all day long. After collecting the items from one list, I was required to stack and wrap these items on a wooden pallet to be shipped. Then I was to go get another packing order and start over again. I shouldn't have to tell you; this became repetitive and monotonous very quickly. This job was more mentally draining than physically taxing because these days would start at 9 AM and could end at 9 PM doing the same thing over and over. After the first 12-hour day, I had another one of those moments that pop up in life. I had to ask myself, "Do you want to do this?". "Not really!" But this was a test of my mental will. I couldn't let this beat me. It was less about what I was actually doing and more about overcoming the feeling of being uncomfortable in a space outside of sports.

I showed up day after day. Just like any muscle I had ever worked out; my mental endurance began to improve. Twelve hours began to feel like ten and I was able to maintain a better pace. I was able to maintain a better attitude. The thought of quitting subsided. It was replaced by the idea of "Every hour I'm here, is more money in my pocket." I was only making $9.00 an hour. In comparison, some of my classmates had internships dishing out $34.00/hr. That's what we can't do, compare ourselves to others. We have to understand that we all don't travel the same path. I was going in a different direction and this just happened to be the lane I was in for the moment.

In many of Milt's crash courses in mental endurance he would tell me that "When you get tired, the mind is the first thing to go." Can you think when you get tired? When you are so focused on keeping your body going, it's hard to remember your responsibilities on a particular play. When your lungs are empty, your legs are trembling, your chest is pounding, with six seconds left on the clock, and your team needs you to make a play, can you focus? Can you come to the line, read the defense, make your adjustments, and execute? After you have done all those things, can you focus on the ball in the air and make the play? That is where your mental endurance rises to the forefront. That is where the true greatness lives.

As I became accustomed to the circumstances, I also found my workout flow. This year was going to be my last chance to show what I had. I wanted to lead my team to a conference championship. There was no space for excuses.

The day started at 6 am with a hearty egg and sausage breakfast. I walked into the gym at 7 am where I would meet one of my coworker's named Broderick. Broderick was in his late 30's. He was jailhouse swole. All he ever wore were wife beaters. He wore them in the gym and to work. Broderick would put weight on machines and bars that I thought were inconceivable. When you train with someone more adept in a particular area, you are bound to get stronger. We would leave the gym and make it to work before 9am, knock out a workday, then get home around 9:00pm. As soon as I got home, I hit the run hills in the neighborhood. My favorite hill was a mile away from the house and about 200 meters long. Sprinting that hill six times then running the mile back to my cousin's house was a death defying. However, when you have your eyes on the target every step has a purpose beneath it. When I finally got back to Uncle Wayde's house, I made up some ab or hip flexor workout. Then came my favorite part of the day, when I slid into bed and closed my eyes. It seemed that as soon as I would get truly comfortable and doze off, suddenly my alarm would go off and it was time to do it all over again.

Once the week was over, I went back to my parents' side of town and trained with Milt on Saturday and Sunday morning. Sunday evening, I headed back to Uncle Wayde's house to do the week over again. I was always drained. It stopped being fun, but I just kept hearing "With the first pick in the 2011 NFL Draft, the Carolina Panthers select Cam Newton!" Reliving that moment reminded me that the dream was tangible. I just had to work for it.

Looking back at what I used to do, it seems crazy. At times I doubt my ability to do it all over again. When you get so engulfed in a dream or goal that is flooded with passion, you will do things you couldn't fathom putting yourself through. But in that mental space you'll do them without even thinking about it. Even if you don't know if it's the right direction, we have to believe that doing as much you can with your passion, is better than not doing anything at all. Even if you find out you are doing the wrong things, you will learn lessons about yourself to take with you as you correct your course. Stretch yourself toward your passion and see what life can teach you. Life is trial and error. The only real wrong thing to do is to do nothing at all. Some people get so caught in planning and trying to do things in the right way and in the right order they forget the most important thing about growth. "The doing!"

HOW BAD DO WE WANT IT?

I wanted a ring. I wanted the NFL. But, one thing I have learned about any sport and ultimately, the game of life is, "you can't do it alone." I understood that I couldn't attain either of these without my team. I can't snap the ball, block, or throw the ball to myself. Football is a team sport. If you don't bring your teammates along, then winning is not your ultimate goal. Having this in mind, I began to call and check with the coaches. I checked on my teammates to see what kind of work they were putting in at school.

It was very disheartening to hear that the other upper-class receivers that were on campus and in summer school had the worst attendance to football activities. We all expected them to be the leaders without me there. When I heard this disappointing news, I called them both on my lunch break. I paced around the parking lot as my ears were filled with excuse after excuse. "I have to work!" "The workouts are at bad times!" "I don't think what they are doing is going to help me!" "I'm going to be in shape when camp comes around." All these excuses shocked me because none of us had ever experienced a winning season as Aggies. This was our last run at this thing, and we are making excuses not to prepare. My pops used to use this saying when I was young, and excuses would flow out of my mouth like a river with no dam. "You can find 1,000 excuses not to do something, but all you need is one reason, to do it!"

At another point in my life, I learned that "Excuses are monuments of nothing. They build bridges to know where. Those who use these tools of incompetence seldom become anything but nothing at all."

Or more famously, "Excuses are like assholes, everybody has one, and only you know what comes from them."

Whichever one locks in the point for you, go write it down. Keep it somewhere you can see it, so it can remind you to watch what comes out of your mouth.

My teammates could tell I was pissed. I asked if they even wanted to go out as MEAC champions. I told them about my work schedule. It was not to show them up, but to impress upon them that whatever is important to a man he will make time for it. I expressed to them that our team was young, yet again this year. The young boys needed to see what it looks like to put in the work to grab the goal. I also expressed that Aggie Pride was real to me and that we weren't doing this just for us. We are going to be the foundation. We would be remembered for digging into the pain of A&T football's darkest hour and pouring the foundation for the future we dreamed of. I wanted to put some RESPECK back on the name of "North Carolina A&T." Filled with truth in their voices they both said they understood and would do better, and these men kept their word.

After six weeks at home were up, I hit the road headed back to Greensboro for summer school. It was my last year at A&T. My coworkers sent me off with an office party and they each expressed in their own way how they appreciated my effort. In the process of working hard, I developed relationships. In a short amount of time, I earned the respect from everyone I came in contact with. We joked, talked about family, talked about where we came from, and about life aspirations. What I have found, is the fastest way to earn a person's respect is to show them your work ethic. The fastest way to develop a friend is to show them that you genuinely care about them as a person. It's almost as if those simple traits are magnetic and people connect with them. The experience working for and with my uncle that summer has had a lasting impact on me. I left feeling like a better follower, a better leader, and a better person from those six weeks. I was also more ready than I had ever been and equipped with the added perspective to go back to school to "get this work!"

Every situation we find ourselves in can add value to the person we are striving to become. It may be as simple as realizing how best to utilize the hours in the day. Maybe it is learning how to find a reason to show up every day, even when what you are doing isn't what you truly want to do. There is growth in everything you decide to find growth in. Can you see the opportunity you have today?

CHAPTER 41 - FIFTH YEARS THE CHARM

At some point in the spring, I realized that I could not run away from the challenge our new situation presented. I was Aggie born into the opportunity to continue to chase after the man I dreamed to be. I was Aggie bred through the struggle, the grind, and the growth to stand tall day in and day out. I decided that I would finish my career and graduate in the place that allowed me the space to find my way. The place that presented me with the challenges that molded me into who I had become. I decided that when I died, I was going to be Aggie dead. I quit my search and prepared to give all I had to the legacy. Returning for my fifth year, all I had, was what they were going to get.

We were in a unique situation, but a position we knew entirely too well. Our new coaching staff had not recruited any of the returning players. For all of us it was like starting over. Just because you were a senior didn't mean you would play. Though I did not like how they came in and disrespected the effort we had put forth amidst the circumstances we were dealt, I was not about to let the way I felt affect my performance. No matter how you look at it, I needed to impress them to keep after my goals.

This year's conditioning test was a completely new recipe. For an appetizer, it consisted of 6 ½ laps on the track which equates 1.625 miles. We had to run it in under 12 minutes. That is not a blistering pace, but it was not a stroll in the park either. The trick for a run like that is consistency. Some guys get out too fast and that monkey jumps on their back for a long ride. Some guys try to start off slow and get behind the clock. This forces you to exert too much energy to possibly catch the clock and like I said, this was an appetizer. Running a consistent race will put you in position to not only finish, but to finish strong. Running that consistent race does not just happen on race day. It comes from your consistent preparation. It can be 20 other guys on the track running fast or running slow, but it's you in your lane, on your track, running your race. This conditioning test sounds a bit like life when you think about it. Consistency is how you find long term success.

Out of the 90 guys only six of us completed that portion of the test on time. After the appetizer we were served with the main course, sixteen 110-yard sprints in the grass. We had to run all these in under 15 seconds. There was technique to these as well. Get out fast and find your stride. You should finish consistently around 14 seconds. If you run the first six all out, you'll end up like me as a freshman. If you start off too slow, you'll be fighting to catch the clock every rep and your legs will be shot. Though in this shorter race you have to get out fast, your overall strategy must remain consistent. Get out, find your stride, and again run your own race. Don't let what's going on around you divert you from your plan.

When all the heavy breathing, cramping, pulled hamstrings, and blurred vision had subsided, only three of my teammates and I were able to finish both runs within the allotted times. A lot of my teammates weren't able to complete the test, let alone pass it. It was so bad that the coaches canceled the individual conditioning punishments they had planned to dish out throughout camp and just conditioned the entire team.

Though I was one of the only guys who passed the conditioning test, that workload on day one had me on the edge of my bed that night, asking myself the question ......again. "Is this what you really want to do?" Four years of a lack of success individually and as a team. Seeing hundreds of guys come in and out. Was destroying my body, draining my spirit, and breaking down my mind worth it? Was the hit my grades took worth it?

I went to sleep that night with that question on my mind. My answer wouldn't come until 6 AM the next morning when the coaches came through the hallways yelling and banging on the doors. Sitting up in the same place I was contemplating the previous night I thought "It's not about how you feel now! All the time and effort you have put in makes it worth it. The scholarship you earned makes it worth it. The confidence you stand tall with makes it worth it. The brothers you earned in the struggle makes it worth it. The life lessons learned within the grind makes it worth it."

Bruises heal. No matter how depleted or broken down you get in a situation, know your mind is like any other part of the body. It stretches and strengthens. Understanding that, the next time you are faced with adversity, your mind is prepared for more weight. "Now stand up lean forward and put one foot in front of the other."

On day two, when we finally reached the field to play, the coaches had a surprise waiting for us. They had divided up the field into stations, with each station having its own challenge. No one said anything but we all knew what was going down. We went through warm-ups as if it were any other day. Once that was over, the shriek of a brand new whistle, fresh out the wrapper pierced our ears. Followed by Coach Prince's bellowing voice shouting, "WE GOT COOOUUUUNNNTTYYYY FAAAIIIRRR.

County Fair (n. /v.) - a series of drills meant to test your agility, speed, coordination, explosion, and whatever other attribute listed on a Madden player rating. The purpose is to get you tired as hell and see how your mind responds.

Every version of "What the ...!" echoed around the field. As a team, we were already mentally defeated before we even started. From the first whistle, my frustration showed through. As I looked around the field, 99% of the 90 players on the field were coasting through the drills. I usually don't say 100% of anything because some part of someone might have been giving it their all. They were just already slow, so I couldn't distinguish them from all of us loafers.

We went through about three stations before that crispy whistle sang out again. It was followed by "START IT OVER!" Followed by more "What the's." Of course, everyone trotted over to the station they began with and started the whole process over again.

If we didn't turn the switch to the "on" position, we would probably do these same drills for the next 3 hours. If we believed we could become MEAC Champions we could not afford to half-ass the first practice of the year. This was a day to set the tone and right now our volume was on low. We were setting the tone for another senior class that came in losers, to leave the same way.

All of that flooded through my mind as I slowly trotted to the first drill. I had seen four classes of seniors walk off the field in their last game as an Aggie with their heads down, defeated. My class was determined to change that storyline and some simple "County Fair" wasn't about to destroy our momentum before it even had a chance to develop.

Not a word was said out loud, but as the whistle rang out again. The tempo was blazing. We fired off the ball, dropped to the ground, rolled in the dirt, whatever the drill required we did it and we did it hard. The younger guys caught on quickly and turned up their intensity until the entire team was going ham in every drill. You could feel the energy as if it were physically pushing you. When we finally completed all nine stations, we were tired as hell. In the same instance, we were hype as hell, begging for more. The mind governs the body.

After we completed "County Fair," we were permitted to start practice. It was short because we wasted so much time on the front end, but we were still relieved when the final whistle sounded off, we all began to make our way to Coach Harper to hear how not good we were today. Instead, we were beckoned to the goal line. "WE GOT PERFECT SPRINTS," Coach Prince yelled out.

Perfect sprints - Consisting of nine lines across the goal line, ten men deep. Every man at the front of the line, must align in a 3-point stance behind the goal line and await his whistle. Once the whistle blew, the person in the front of the line must run a 40-yard sprint all the way through the 40 yard line. The man behind him then places his hand in the ground and the process was continued until each man in each line has sprinted 40 yards.

Rules: You must run through the line before slowing up or that rep doesn't count. If one person false starts before the whistle, that rep doesn't count. If one person's hand wasn't behind the line that rep doesn't count. If a coach perceived one person as loafing, then that rep doesn't count. A rep not counting did not mean that we stopped that rep. It meant that all 90 players finished their rep, but that rep did not go toward our total number needed to complete.

The more rules you broke, the more in shape you became or the more tired you were, depending on how you looked at it. "We got eight" Coach Prince bellowed. Sounds easy enough, right? When you're on a team and you have to rely on every man to do their job, you no longer give your all for purely personal gains. Perfect sprints are the perfect test of who is willing to put their feelings, pain, fatigue, and emotions to the side and give it up for the team.

We started well. All 90 players crossed the line in good enough form for the coaches to count the first one. After that things got off the tracks quickly. The whistle just continued to blow. So and so, didn't put their hand down. So and so, didn't finish through the line. So and so, started with his foot on the line. "THAT DON'T COUNT!!!"

At one point, it became routine for us to hear the whistle followed by "THAT DON'T COUNT!" They were messing with us. I remember the coaches huddled up joking around during a rep not paying us any attention. We still heard "THAT DON'T COUNT." By the time we were able to get eight perfect sprints to count, my count was up to 37 attempts.

Finally, the physical part of day two was over. The coaches wanted complete team discipline. They wanted us in better shape than anyone we faced, and we weren't there yet. We didn't have total commitment to the new team philosophy, but we did show resolve. I say that because not one person quit. Every year prior, at least one person would walk off the field and out of the locker room to never be seen again. "You can't quit after you went through all of that."

I talked to a couple of coaches as camp went on and they told me day one and two were to see who would mentally break. Now it was time to be a better football team.

One thing we knew about our coaching staff was they won everywhere they went and winning was the mission. I didn't care what it looked like. As much as I hated hearing Coach Harper tell us we weren't very good day in and day out, I was starting to buy into what he was selling. He was selling the system, the mindset, and the process. "How is what I am doing helping us?" That was the question. No longer was I in search of 70 receptions, 1,000 yards and 10 touchdowns. My mentality shifted to a greater purpose. Now the mentality was "How can I take advantage of as many opportunities as I can, to help the team win?"

If you were climbing a mountain you had never climbed with a group of people and you ran into a guide that had scaled this mountain several times, do you think it's a good idea to take his advice? Is it a better idea to follow him up the mountain? What if he told you that for you to stand at the summit of the mountain and look down over the world in triumph, you needed every person in the group. That's what it takes to win a championship. You should add value and growth to others around you. You can climb a hill by yourself any day, but when you get to the top of that hill, look up. The champions will be waving down at you from the mountain. The question is do you want to be a champion?

CHAPTER 42 - YOU AREN'T VERY GOOD! OK, NOW WHAT!

Coach Harper ended just about every practice with the same words. "We are not very good; we have to get better. We aren't close right now. We aren't a very good football team." Imagine after every day of going out and putting everything you had on the field, at work, or in the classroom you are told by the person you have decided to follow, "You're not very good." Steadily diminishing all the effort, time, blood, sweat, and literal tears you put in. How are you supposed to feel about coming back to work to give it your all?

This is where perspective is important. What most people fail to realize is that you have the wheel. You direct your ship. The easy road is self-pity and complaining. It takes no effort or focus to throw a pity party. It can feel natural in the same way a baby finds comfort in crying because it didn't get its way.

Another path will take in awareness that may be a little scary. What if you aren't as amazing as you think you are? What if you aren't as great as you can be? Whether it's from within or from an outside entity viewing you objectively, it takes some real honest awareness to grow. If you don't realize that growth needs to occur, then there is a good chance you won't do the work necessary to do it. Accept that there is a deficiency within you and decide to show up the next day to work on it. It may take an effort that is uncomfortable, but there is growth and power this way.

There was tension between the players and the staff initially. But, as slow as a 400lb. lineman running a 400 meter sprint, we began to realize that Coach Harper was the "mirror on the wall" we needed. He was the truth we shied away from. He caused us to critique ourselves tougher, govern ourselves harder, and become mentally stronger.

Every day of my career at A&T, it felt like I had to work hard to earn the next day. Even after I had earned my scholarship. Coach Harper's regime taught me that that wasn't enough. They also taught me that I had more than even I thought I did within me. This season was us seniors last opportunity to solidify our legacy within the 110-year history of our football program. The stars were aligning in a sense. We had a coaching staff that knew what it took to win and with Lewis coming back from his injury, the best passing QB to come through A&T in over a decade. We had an experienced offensive line, a superstar running back, and a nationally ranked defense. The only question was my group. Could we attack teams down the field and be consistent?

Camp went on and the coaches got a better understanding of what they had — especially our Offensive Coordinator, Joe Pizzo, and our receiver coach, Shaun Hunter. Coach Pizzo was a tall, middle-aged white guy. He had straight slicked back jet black hair and matching sunglasses. Picture any mafia movie. He is the guy that walks into the corner store wearing dark shades inside to collect protection payments. He walked slow and deliberate. He spoke the same way.

Coach Pizzo snagged my attention when he told me to watch some film of a receiver named Dobson Collins. By chance, while working with Milt one summer, I had the opportunity to train with Dobson. I knew Dobson had gotten an opportunity in the NFL with the San Francisco 49ers, Philadelphia Eagles, and the Baltimore Ravens. Dobson, who played for Coach Pizzo when he coached at Gardner Webb University, had career numbers under Pizzo his senior year — setting the stage for Dobson's professional opportunities. Coach Pizzo told me he wanted to get me the ball as he did with Dobson. I noticed something else while watching Dobson's highlights. Even though Dobson was getting the ball on the highlight I saw his fellow receivers running open. To me this was a sign that his schemes could help us win because everyone could eat.

After watching the film, Coach Pizzo had me locked in. The icing on the cake came one day when I was sitting in his office, continuing to get to know him. I expressed to him that my favorite team growing up was the Detroit Lions. In my google search of Coach Pizzo, I saw he had played for the Detroit Lions during a short stint in the NFL. What he told me next blew my mind. He told me his locker was right next to my favorite player of all time, Barry Sanders. After that talk with him, I felt like *The Secret* of the universe had once again placed someone in my life to grow me in my journey. I went home and got to studying. The excitement for my senior year intensified even more because I felt we finally had the situation I had been yearning for. We had the opportunity to spread the ball around and show all of our talents. We had the guy calling the plays in our corner and he trusted us. As rigid as he could be sometimes, it was easy to play for Coach Pizzo because I felt he had our best interest at heart.

Coach Shaun Hunter was our receiver coach. At first sight he is an awkward, uncharismatic white guy. He didn't carry himself very confidently. He probably had the most substantial social gap to close amongst any coach I have ever come in contact with. Coach Hunter had never played receiver before and was never a really good football player. When he shared that with us, to me it showed us something meaningful. Even though we clowned him for it, he showed us from the jump that he would shoot us straight. He was willing to have vulnerable conversations. He set the tone, creating space for everyone in our group to be honest. A little too honest sometimes. But this guy is the epitome of the saying "Don't judge a book by its cover"!

After we got past his appearance, background, and awkwardness we found that this man was committed to doing everything in his power and beyond to get us ready to be successful on and off the field. We didn't realize at the moment, but he was doing the best he could to get us mentally ready for life. He would do any and everything for us. He requested the best from us, for us. He didn't just preach he cared for us, but he showed it. He was a young white guy on a Historically Black University campus engulfed in a new culture. He was able to adapt and "he did his thing"! Now and then I would see him walking through campus and I'd ask him where he was headed to. He would always say he was going to check on some player to make sure they were in class.

He didn't have to do that. He could have called or text them and left it at that. He literally went the extra mile. Maybe he was just doing his job, but I appreciated him even though he was never out looking for me in particular. He was out to hold us accountable for life, not just football.

Dealing with Coach Hunter I can honestly say I had never been so mentally prepared to go into games as I was that year. He broke down coverages. He spotted looks that might have been shown once in four or five games. I specifically remember a look he called out in preparation for the Appalachian State, which resulted in a 30-yard reception for me. "When you're in the slot, and you see the safety roll down not looking at you, don't worry about him as you run past him on the vertical, you may feel free. You are not free. The cornerback outside you has shown in Cover 3 he will squeeze the seam. You won't see him but know that he is coming." During the game, it occurred verbatim. Once the safety passed me, I knew I couldn't just run under the ball. I had to go up and get it. As soon as my hands touched the ball, I felt the corner. He was precisely where Hunter told me he would be. He scraped across my arms and hit me in the back. A big play but more importantly a confidence builder between coach and player.

WE READY?

Early on usually the offense ran into a lot of different issues. For a while it felt like we were tormented and taunted day in and day out by the defense. To top off every practice hearing from the judge and the jury, Coach Harper, "We aren't a very good football team."

When it comes to any drastic change to improve yourself, know that the results tend to get worse before they get better. Understand that this is ok. You are moving in a way neither your body, nor your mind is accustomed to.

Let's stick with the geological analogies. You have been hiking up a hill and you have reached the top. In that moment you are excited about your accomplishment. You feel comfortable with where you have arrived. Suddenly you realize you are just on the foothills of a mountain. Though you have reached success before, in order to scale the mountain, you're going to have to develop a new set of attributes.

Climbing a mountain takes a few more skills, a bit more endurance, a lot more resilience, and a more intense attention to the details than it did to walk up your hill. Initially, you are going to struggle. The task of climbing this mountain is going to be daunting. Part of you is going to want to go back to that little hill that you know top to bottom. Recognize your hill peaks just high enough to see the next hill in the distance. To see the vast possibilities for yourself and what the world has to offer, attack the mountain. Even if success doesn't come your way initially.

Yeah, you're going to struggle and trip. You might cramp and possibly fall in what's new. If you keep showing up, keep working, keep trying, keep using your team, you will adopt a new set of skills. Skills that will propel you step-by-step, decision by decision up this mountain. The tortoise won the race with the hare by focused consistency. Ignore distractions and focus on the next step, the next play, the next class, the next challenge. If you focus on what's right in front of you every day one day you will notice that you are standing atop your mountain looking out over the landscape at the vast number of possibilities to go after with your new skills and experiences. You will also be able to look down at the peak of the little hill that at one time was your comfort zone.

Where a lot of people lose is when they run into an obstacle on their climb. This is when it gets tough, and you can't see what's on the other side. They run back to their little hill. I can promise you if you stick with the mountain, the new knowledge, and skills you earn from your fight with adversity will support you as you reach heights even you couldn't not have envisioned. When you reach the top of your mountain, you'll realize your success is in the foothills of an even greater mountain. This time though, you know the process that awaits you to reach the top of this new challenge. This is only because you did not run back to the comfort zone of your little hill. Overcoming discomfort starts before you ever lift a finger. It's a decision to begin and then decisions continue.

After a couple of days of us sticking to the process and getting blasted by the defense, the offense started clicking. It was more than plays on the field. We started understanding playing for one another. We found the fun again. This was the turning point that gave us momentum moving up the mountain of the 2011 season.

WHERE MY HITTAS AT

I told you about my altercations as a freshman. Not once did I say my offensive teammates came to my side in those fights. Never did I say my actions started a team brawl. It was always me one on one or one on the sea of blue. This year I noticed a difference during one evening practice under the lights. I got into a brief little scuffle with one of our safeties. He was mad because I cracked him and knocked him on his neck. As much as defensive players like to hit, they equally don't like to get hit. He took offense and came jawing at me on the sideline. We went back and forth for a quick second. Even though I had retired from fighting my teammates, I knew where this was headed. I was going to have to come out of retirement for this one.

As I was fixing my fist, it was as if the sun came back out. I was blinded by a swarm of yellow jerseys surrounding me. This fool then tried to rush the crowd and swung a wild punch. He must have been blinded by the wall of yellow because his aim was off. I watched his wild punch miss me in slow motion. I did as any proper gentleman should, in these circumstances, I returned fire, but I guess neither one of us was seeing straight cause we both missed each other's battleships.

The headline wasn't "Wallace Miles vs. Isaiah Martin". The real story was my offensive line, running backs, and other receivers rushed in. They had my front, my sides, and my back. Little things like that told me we were becoming WE. In the moment I was mad he tried me, but I was smiling on the sideline after everyone dispersed because I knew I finally had a squad that had my back as strong as I believed I had theirs.

Practice felt different. More people came out day in and day out to honestly get better. For years I watched many of my teammates come out to practice to get by, collect their scholarship, wear a jersey, and get the girls that come with being a football player. This felt different; it was beginning to feel right.

No matter how hard we battled or how well we played, each day we were continually greeted with "We are not a very good football team!" By now I believe it was starting to have the desired effect on us. These words no longer demoralized us but instead ignited us. They became a daily challenge. We knew we weren't very good. If we came out here and wasted a day, then we didn't even have a chance of becoming a good team. Every day we chased words we had never come across.

As camp ended, though we weren't a good team, we realized we had grown as a team and as brothers in this journey. We were healthy and we were excited to hit someone else.

CHAPTER 43 - LAST CHANCE U

First up was Virginia University of Lynchburg. A program playing its first football game in 57 years. As a senior and a captain, I took it upon my shoulders to give my team that *pep talk* you see in the movies when everyone goes crazy. After our last practice before the game, the scene was set as I stepped in the middle of the huddle. As the silent leader of the team who led by example, pulling people to the side for that one on one leadership, no one expected what came next.

I had been thinking about what I would say and how I would say it. While reading an article earlier in the week from VUL, I saw a repetitive theme. They thought they were going to beat us because we were supposedly a losing program. This pissed me off, but I quickly realized I needed to use that energy. This team was pieced together literally with young men they found on the street and they dared to think they were going to beat us. Looking back on it now, "What else were they supposed to think?" But in the moment, I took it as the greatest insult.

My teammates didn't even know it, but it was about to go down. I stepped in the middle of the huddle, "I got something to say!" I took a second while everyone quieted down. I pulled out a folded-up piece of paper from inside my tights. It was the article I had read.

"VUL has been disrespecting us! They haven't had a team in 57 years and in the newspaper, they said they are going to beat us in our house."

Looking at Mike Mayhew, "They say our running backs are soft."

Looking over at Alex Harper "They say our offensive line can't block."

Then to Derek Gould "Man they said our receivers can't get open."

"These fools even said our defense can't stop nobody" eyes darting to every blue jersey I could find. "They said we don't have a quarterback." as I locked eyes with Lewis.

"This is my last go-round and I'm pissed!" They didn't feel the pain we fought through day one of camp. I want to make them want to quit football."

Then I set it off with our A&T war song:

Me: "I said I would not be a Dra-gon"

Aggies: "Yeaaaaaaaah"

Me: "I said I would not be a Dra-gon."

Aggies: "Yeaaaaaah"

Me: "Imma tell you the reason why!"

Aggies: "Whyyyyyy?"

All together: "Cause I've been an AGGIE all my life. I'll be an AGGIE till I die, hey! hey! Hey!"

"SOOOOO HARD, SO HARD, SO HARD TO BE AN AGGIE."

" SO HARD, SO HARD, SO HARD TO BE AN AGGIE."

" SO HARD, SO HARD, TO BE AN A&T, AGGIE WOOOOOOOOO (Ric Flair style)!"

It got the desired reaction. The excitement and intensity echoed out across the field. At that moment you could feel the closeness of this team. The enthusiasm for the season and excitement we had for each other showed bright that day. We were ready!

The next morning in the hotel I sat up on the edge of the bed to speak with God. I told him I appreciated him for keeping me healthy during camp and the opportunities he had brought me through and into; new coaches, revitalized teammates, and the abilities he had cultivated in me. To think if I had listened to "them", "we" would not be here today. I would not be me today. Finally, I asked him to be with me in this game and to lead this team to a victory.

The team ate breakfast together, followed by a meeting to go through any last-minute corrections or questions. Then it was game time. My last season as an Aggie was here.

GO TIME

My team selected me as a captain for the season and as I watched the referee's coin flicker in the bright sun as it flipped, I thought "It doesn't matter what it lands on. We are ready for whatever." We had no fear of what they were bringing to the table because of the work we put in.

The drums, the trumpets, cymbals, and tubas roared as the band began to play our intro. I ran down to the team dove on top of the huddle, yelling "It's time! It's time!" I loved running through that tunnel to the thunder of our band. As I ran out this time, it felt different. The realization that the countdown of my time as an Aggie football player had started. Every play and every moment was more precious than the one before. Everything had to count. If you think about it, that should be our mindset no matter how much time we have left.

As I trotted on the field to the beat of the Blue and Gold Marching Machine, I was locked in. Though we came out with enormous energy, the game started slowly for both teams. We were killing ourselves with mistakes and they just had no answer for our defense. We went into half up 10-0, but we felt it should have been 28-0 already. We were playing down to their level and I was pissed about it. I was boiling to make a play and on the first play of the half, Coach Pizzo called the play. I looked at Lew and he looked right back at me. We knew what was about to happen. Lewis hiked the ball, took a 5 step drop and a hop. Just as he was about to get hit, he let it fly.

At the same time, he let it go, I put my foot in the ground at the top of my corner post route. The safety saw the ball at the same time I saw it. The difference between us was he was falling to the ground. Lewis hit me in stride streaking down the middle of the field for a 52-yard touchdown. The stands erupted and the band blasted. The biggest piece of the celebration to me was when I turned around and saw the party my teammates and coaches were having on the sideline. From that moment on, we played at our level and demolished them 38-7. It was a team win; everyone seemed to be making plays. I finished with a career high seven receptions for 152 yards and that touchdown, that seemed to be the spark.

Once again, I was blessed to be able to share that success with my foundation, my support team, my family. Most of them had made the trip up from Atlanta to join me at the start of my last ride. They filled me with their love. I looked at my parents and I knew why. I looked at my sister, Claudia and I knew why. I looked at my aunts and my cousins, and I knew why I did it!

When the celebration was all said and done, I ended up on the edge of my bed that night, talking to God again. Thanking God for guiding us to the exact start we had prayed for and worked for.

CHAPTER 44 - THE SUGAR IN THE SALT

The next week we were headed up to Boone, North Carolina to face off with a perennial D1-AA juggernaut in Appalachian State. This was a program that had won three National Championships in the last decade. On paper we had no chance. The way we prepared that week and the attitude we took down to Boone, NC, you couldn't tell we were an underdog. Pregame was normal. The excitement was there. The atmosphere was thumping'. Even with all the craziness going on when we stepped out together, preparing to charge onto the field, I felt a focus come over me. All the chaos around me and I was in the midst, quiet. "Lead today" kept resonating in my head.

As much excitement and fire that we came out with, App. State came out and punched us in the mouth. They scored 14 quick points in the first quarter and went into the half down 21-0. As we walked off the field, I had seen the faces I was looking into before. They were saying, "here we go again." I could tell some of us had checked out. We had an uphill battle, and it appeared we were giving up. We couldn't go down this road again. We hadn't come out here to get embarrassed like this. The quiet leader snapped with a rage I had never unleashed before.

"Bruh! We say we work harder than anyone in the country! Today is the time to prove it. They are no different than any one of us. Let them feel you this half. On offense we gotta know what we are doing. The plays are there, let's make'm. They are not just for you. If you are truly your brother's keeper make'm for your brother! Defense! Bang'm! Let them feel us all week long! They are privileged. Be grimy. Let's GO! If you step out of this locker room in this blue and gold, understand giving up is not an option!"

The energy was not like it was at the beginning of the game, but it had been resuscitated. We broke it down in the locker room and charged back onto the field. We were only down three scores with a half to play, but the first drive set us up with some momentum to make a monumental comeback.

Lewis hit me on a 31 yard out and up. We were set up on their 44-yard line. We ran a running play that gained us four yards. On that running play, I decided to test out the DB in front of me. What I observed was his feet weren't very organized. After the play I ran to Lew and said, "Lets hit him deep, he got bad feet." Yea I was dropping bars in the middle of the game. We called a time out. We walked over to Coach Hunter, who was on the headset with Coach Pizzo. Hunter said, what are you thinking? Immediately I said, "Let's go deep." Hunter looked at Lew and Lew gave him the nod. Coach Pizzo was listening to the whole conversation and called the play. Twins Left 70 Play-Action 99. As we ran to the line, I tried to play it cool, trying to act like nothing was going on, but in my head, I kept saying "It's going down!"

REALITY IS BITTERSWEET

At the line, I looked in at Lew and just like the previous week he was looking back at me. We both knew what was about to happen. "Set Hut" I exploded off the line and closed the gap on the corner. I gave him a move Milt made famous in Canada, dubbed the "dead leg." The DB's feet stopped just enough for me to accelerate past him. Lew put up a pretty ball that hung up high and came down just as nice. It hit me in stride, gliding into the end zone. As if a bomb went off in our section of the stadium the fans and cheerleaders leapt off their feet. My teammates and I celebrated in the end zone, but when I looked back to our sidelines it was utter chaos. The whole sideline was rocking including our coaches and trainers. The comeback was on. We knew we could play with this nationally ranked team. Sometimes all it takes is a spark. One success to ignite belief in the unbelievable.

We had the feeling that we could complete this comeback. The energy was back. The communication was alive. We wanted more from ourselves. But, as much as we wanted it and believed in ourselves, reality is reality. Appalachian State was a more developed program and had a more developed team at that time. We went on to lose the game 58-6. We got out schemed, out hit, outran, and out played. That's the reality when a prepared team faces one that is "not very good." On the biggest stage, A&T had been on in a decade, we took it on the chin.

As frustrated as we were with the loss, there was something sweet at the core of this rotten experience. Remember, lessons don't always show themselves on the cover. Normally they are found in the pages that follow, we just have to look for them. App. St. was the better team. Sometimes you are going to face an opponent who is better prepared than you on that day, but be observant in defeat. See the difference between you and your opponent. See your opponent's strengths and weaknesses, learn from them both. Store that knowledge in a file cabinet of your mind and be ready to utilize what you learned about yourself and what you learned about your opponent in preparation for future battles. Defeat requires you to look in the mirror. Take a look at yourself. What did we do wrong? What do we need to improve on? Go back to the laboratory and concoct the elixir.

Of course, Coach Harper said, "We weren't very good," we sucked our teeth like six-year-olds, and quietly packed up our bags to get on the bus. We lost and I was in a pretty bad mood. My smile was brought back as I walked out the locker room and again caught the eyes of my family. The same people who were there for the triumph the week before were there as I walked out of one of the worst losses I had ever experienced. They were there to support me on my journey in football, but also my journey through life. Recognize those people who are in your corner on your best days as well as your worst.

Embrace those people that believe in you. Gravitate to those people who have a genuine positive interest in your growth. In life we will have to discern those who are truly there for us. Your worst days illuminate those people very well. That day it's not in you, they speak it in you. When you've been beaten down, they reach down and help you to your feet. When you finally succeed, they lift you on their shoulders and they celebrate your journey.

When the time comes, remember what those people in your life gave to you and pay it forward. Pay it to someone who your love and support can strengthen. Remember the uplifting feeling it gave you. Try it out! There is a surprise in it for you when you do.

CHAPTER 45 - FOCUS SPACE

We took a beating. After learning the lessons from the lost and another week of practice, we were back in the fight. As long as you stay in the fight, you will have an opportunity to win. You only truly lose when you give up and stop fighting. The next challenge for us were the Chanticleers of Coastal Carolina and their top prospect Lance Peoples, who was later drafted in the 5th round of the NFL Draft.

Coach Pizzo was familiar with Peoples from his previous clashes when he coached at Gardner Webb. He admittedly was fearful of going at Peoples, but to me this was a chance for me to see where I stood against real NFL talent. I wasn't afraid and was riding a wave of confidence from having 300 plus yards after the first two games of the season.

Coach Pizzo was playing to win. He wasn't worried about the ego trip I was attempting to take off on. As minor as this lesson may seem, it will prove enormous when it comes to your success, that of your team, your business, and your family. When you have more than yourself to lead toward success, getting caught too deep in how great you are and allowing your ego to control your decisions can lead to the demise of the whole.

Maneuver in a way that WE win. The growth and success of the team is what truly matters. Landon Peoples was as advertised. We didn't see each other much because of the greater good. I finished with eight receptions for 88 yards and a TD but, we lost again. The offense might not have performed as well as we did if Coach Pizzo had listened to a nearsighted young man on an ego trip. Though we lost the game, our offense showed it was picking up momentum. I always wondered how that battle with Lance Peoples would have played out, but for the bigger picture "Good call, coach!"

Starting 1-2 was not how I saw my senior year, especially after all the growth we had seen. Coach Harper was honest when he said: "We aren't very good." We weren't a very good football team. We had a very long way to go and not much time to get there.

Coach Harper had another saying that seems to be one of the most significant mental concepts I have come across. It sets the foundation for resilience on either end of the spectrum. "When something good happens, keep playing! When something bad happens, keep playing!

Never get too high, never get too low, always hover somewhere in between."

This is the epitome of the next play mentality. Come into every scenario as its own. Nothing that has happened in the past, good, or bad, has any bearing on the execution of the next play. Enter with the same focus every time.

Are you able mute your emotions to think and perform optimally, even after you dropped the ball? Muting is not deleting your feelings. Just like a television remote it is quieting the noise so you can think clearly. Next time you get really happy or really sad, try this. Take three deep breaths and answer the question "What's next?" Coach Harper brought home the principle my parents had been trying to teach me throughout my life.

We must be resilient, even when something good happens. Don't drink the Kool-Aid, because it's never as sweet as we try to make it out to be. Fight the desire to get too excited. Fight the thought of how great you are. As soon as you lose focus for one second, the next game or even the next play, everything could fall apart. Hover in the focus space at all times, the "somewhere in between". We can always celebrate how good we did after the game or after we are champions.

MIRRORED FOCUS

After two back to back losses, as a unit, coaches included we were forced to evaluate ourselves. We had seen this trend before. Two losses could quickly turn into ten. There is a famous line from the Matrix where the character, Switch, faced with the harsh reality that her plug is about to be pulled, and she will die. Her last words were, "Not like this! Not like this!"

Knowing that this could be it and having seen it before, the machine began to churn. We had three games under our belt. Plenty of time to look in the mirror and get a good view of who we actually were. Our strengths and weaknesses were caught on film. They were put on full exhibit for each of our brothers to see. The greatest test was going to be how honest we could be with ourselves. It can be tough to be honest with yourself. To see, recognize, and accept that you are still flawed no matter how much work you have put in is tough. No matter how good you think you are, you have flaws that can be improved upon. Are you human enough to accept this? Are you human enough to work on it?

Where was that fight and brotherhood we developed during camp? Was it for show or was it engraved in the foundation of the monument we had committed to building?

Our senior class came into a program that had the longest losing streak in the nation and team sanctions due to the leadership and ethics of the prior Aggie generation. We had seen every class lose their last homecoming and walk off the field of the last game they would ever play, defeated.

This wasn't our story, and this wasn't going to be our legacy. There will be moments in life where your back is up against the wall. You will have to draw on all your previous experiences, positive or negative to fight your way out. In this moment we had to take a stand. We had to bring that toolbox in one hand and lunch pail in the other.

The renewed focus was evident across the board. Once we began to see ourselves for who we were, we were able to double down on our strengths and dig into our weaknesses. All the talking was out the window and into the wind. We started to inch toward the growth we had been searching for.

Morgan State was up next, and a few familiar faces glared at us from across the field. Coach Thomas had taken a few of his coaches to Savannah State with him. He was the new offensive coordinator. Thomas knew us. He understood our personnel and our abilities. Thomas recruited most of the current players on the team. We were his team, but it didn't matter. They took me completely out of the game with their game plan, but that didn't matter. I ended the game with zero receptions.

This is the moment that the growth we were searching for began to show its face. Leadership often appears in selfless action. We realized that we were running the ball well. We also realized their outside linebackers were undersized. Just like I had done against App St. I told Hunter what I saw, but it wasn't about me getting the ball.

"Coach run it my way."

The number one primadonna receiver, was now requesting to practically be an O-lineman for the betterment of the team. That's a change in mindset. That's a change in culture. That mindset was what Coach Harper was trying to instill in us. "Mike follow me, bruh!"

That's what we did. We ran the ball all game long right at outside linebackers #54 and #32. Between the O-line handling their D-line and the receivers blocking at the second level, we cleared a path for Mike to run for 233 yards and a 78-yard touchdown. This growth led us to a 24-3 win in Baltimore, against a program A&T had not beaten in almost a decade.

On the field, we felt it. When we watched the film, we saw it. There was a heart that hadn't resided in an A&T team

I had played on to this point. It wasn't anything miraculous. Just a steady effort to improve ourselves individually for the collective. For my brothers and I, "Aggie Pride" and the man next to us, became the why. We wanted to hone every skill to make the team successful.

We aimed to prove Coach Harper wrong. We aimed to prove that we were a good football team and at the same time to prove Coach Harper right. Prove that he was the right man for the job, to transform a group of dysfunctional kids into young men with the mentality of winners. Most of all, we aimed to prove that though we were products of our past, we were no longer our past.

Next up were the defending Co-MEAC Champs, the Bethune Cookman Wildcats. The same team that beat us 67-17 on national television the year before. This was personal and it showed on the field early. The defense led the way. Big hit after big hit, noticeably softened the wildcats, turning them into domesticated kittens. Our defense forced three fumbles an interception and held a team that averaged 260 yards on the ground to 5 rushing yards. The offense just came in as a closer and sealed the deal for a 22-3 win. "AGGIE PRIDE" was in full effect.

Live in your focus space so you can be ready and efficient in your lowest failures, as well as your greatest triumphs. Remember, you are you in either scenario and your light can burn bright in either space. I believe in your light, your resilience, and your calm. I believe in you through your journey. When you believe, is when nothing will stop you.

CHAPTER 46 - A GHOE MIRACLE

One day in your journey through this world, it is imperative that you make a pilgrimage to Greensboro, NC in late October for North Carolina A&T's Homecoming. It is an experience of a lifetime. Of course, there is the game which was my main focus for 5 years. The happenings that surround the stadium from Friday night to the early hours of Sunday morning, engulf not only the campus, but the entire city of Greensboro in celebration of a culture within the culture. Positive energy, love, and pride in support of an idea that has transcended generations. Homecoming is the one time of the year where the progeny of our decorated University return home from every corner of the world to celebrate that idea. The idea that people of African descent can organize and gain knowledge about themselves, the world, and develop skills toward becoming self-sufficient members of the greater society. This premise was believed impossible at certain periods of time in this country's past, but North Carolina A&T creates a nurturing environment for this idea to flourish.

Making the yearly pilgrimage back home, thousands of alumni want to see A&T, the school, and the team, in its best form. For seven straight years, they returned to watch their beloved Aggie football team take it on the nose. Losing the game and losing respect on the name of our university. In my 4 years, I had never seen a homecoming victory. A&T had been deprived so long that students and alumni alike had been trained to expect us to lose. They would start the party at the tailgates before the game, take a lap around the stadium to show off their Homecoming outfit and by half time the stands were clear. Everyone was back on the yard continuing the turn-up.

I listened to every senior I had ever played with say they had never won a homecoming game and that it was going to change "this year" as they laced up their cleats for the last time at an A&T homecoming. Every last one of them walked off the field the same as the one before, in defeat.

I had the same ambition to rectify our homecoming drought. I uttered the same words as my brothers before me, but a hint of doubt crept in. We were mentally conditioned to lose "big games". The mental battle to overcome your negative conditionings is a warfare that takes a purpose found deep within.

The day before the game my roommate, starting running back, Mike Mayhew got the call I was expecting a little less than a year earlier. His girlfriend was in labor preparing to have his baby girl in Atlanta. Mike didn't want to miss the birth of his child, but he also didn't want to miss the game. He knew what it meant. He had a decision to make, and I believe he made the right one. He hopped on the road. He drove five hours in the dead of night, to be a part of the first experience of his daughter's life.

Just because our starting running back and half of our offensive statistical production was gone, didn't mean the game would be delayed. We woke the next morning, feeling the excitement of the entire city. The moment had come for us to change the narrative of A&T football. The aroma of the fiery grills filled the air as we approached the stadium. People were cheering and pumping their fist as we drove by getting off the bus. We plunged headfirst into the heart of Aggie nation. The tone was set, the emotion was flowing, and the hype of what was before us had engulfed the locker room. Having all this positive energy surrounding me, I still smelt a faint scent of doubt that permeated through my pads.

As I strapped my shoulder pads up, preparing to go out for pregame warmups, the locker room door swung open. In walked my roommate, the new father, Mike Mayhew. He walked past everyone with a focused determined look on his face and went straight to the training room to get taped. In this moment that shred of doubt that was floating with me, evaporated. Thinking about what this man did to get to Atlanta to experience the "miracle of birth."

Knowing that he had the strength, drive, and loyalty to get back on the road in the early hours of the morning to come fight with his brothers, set me at ease.

From a guy who consistently quit conditioning workouts during the summer, it represented to me that the culture had completed its transformation. A&T was truly on its way back. The pride of the nation and the pride in ourselves once again meant something. We were ALL IN. The birth of his daughter made me think this was a brand new day and a brand new era in A&T football. I laced my cleats up and grabbed my helmet. I confidently walked out of the locker room and stepped into a brand new day reassured that we were more than our past.

When you come from a situation of negativity and continual loss, it is ridiculously hard to completely rid yourself of the doubt that the negative outcome is not around the corner ready to strike. It will be an everlasting battle, but latching on to a symbol that reaffirms where you are headed is a cold spring in the dessert. You will be in a fight for your life, but cherish those instances that aid in replenishing your faith. Doubt will grow like poison ivy, entrapping and infecting your thoughts. It will never go away permanently. We must train our minds to adhere to some greater meaning consistently. What really happens, is you will refocus your sight and see through the doubt, rendering it powerless.

After seeing Mike, I was ready! We were ready. We went out and put a spanking on Delaware State 42-24, with the new father, scoring three touchdowns after traveling over 700 miles in 16 hours. The little monster who was growing into a grown man, Larry, also caught three touchdowns that day. As much as the fans celebrated in the stands, we celebrated in the end zone. My last homecoming wasn't about me. It was about the celebration of WE, AGGIE Football and AGGIE PRIDE.

CHAPTER 47 - SEEING THE TOP, IS NOT THERE

After beating Delaware State, we were ranked number 1 in the conference for the first time in 8 years. All the work appeared to be paying off. We were beginning to synchronize. We were beginning to feel and understand who we were and the roles we fulfilled as a part of the whole. We were beginning to understand who our team was. There was different energy at the facility, on campus, and in the community. We were in a place we had only heard of.

"When something good happens, keep playing. When something bad happens, keep playing."

Something great was happening, but Coach Harper had us still preparing the way we were when we were trying to find ourselves. One thing about football, next week will show how true to the process you are.

The next week we attacked our preparation, watching the film, lifting the weights, and executing at practice. And when it was time to hit the road north to Washington D.C. to play Howard University. We were ready. We knew the atmosphere would be crazy because it was their homecoming. We expected hostile territory, but we felt confident because we put in the work to be ready for whatever they could throw at us.

I guess they were ready for us as well because they jumped out to an early 13-0 lead, in the 1st half. There was a different feel though. When we were down at App St. it felt like we gave up hope. On this day, the look in everyone's eyes said we can still win this. If we had any doubts Coach Harper came in with some simple words, "We are not playing very well, but we can win this game!" followed by "When something bad happens...." "KEEP PLAYING" the team responded.

We came out of the locker room focused. We put together two scoring drives to start the second half. Mike scored on a one yard run. Then Lewis and I connected on a 20-yard touchdown to take the lead going into the 4th quarter. Back and forth punches were thrown all of them seeming to connect. The all out brawl was even when the last whistle blew. Both teams were bleeding, but both still standing in a 28-28 tie.

OVERTIME

We were trained to be resilient. No longer were we pushovers. We were evolving in the moment. If you hit us, we hit back. It was our time. We stepped back in the ring squinting through a cut eye, legs wobbling, and ribs bruised. As soon as the ref said "fight" We were hit hard in the face again. They scored in 6 plays on their first possession. It was up to the offense to counter.

On first down our backup QB rushed for 10 yards to the 15-yard line. Three plays later, on 3rd and 9, Lewis hit me for a 11-yard gain, down to the three yard line. There was no way they could stop us with four downs from the three-yard line.

First down was an incomplete pass to the tight end. "No big deal." Second down we handed the ball to our All-Conference running back. Howard guessed right and stuffed the box for the run, stopping Mike short of the goal line. Third Down. It's funny how all it takes is two plays to change your perspective of being in the same spot. We tried another quick pass that went incomplete. Now it was fourth down. You could feel the panic from our coaches, the stands, and from within ourselves. We were down to our last chance. We had to score. We knew they knew we were going to run the ball. We made the obvious decision. We ran a pass play. This would give Lewis the option to hit the open man or take off and run. Howard was playing chess. They showed like they were going to blitz, but at the snap of the ball the linebackers dropped into the quick passing lanes still spying Lewis. Lewis did as he was supposed to. He scanned his first and second reads. When he realized they were covered he put his head down and took off for the goal line. When he did the linebackers did what they were supposed to do, they pursued.

When they did, I found myself standing right in front of Lewis in the end zone wide open. It was an easy toss. We were set for overtime #2, but Lewis had committed to the run. His head was down ready to deliver and absorb the contact coming his way. The collision occurred at the 1-yard line with two Bison defenders. I could feel how determined he was to score for us. He twisted and turned. He drove his feet into the ground pushing for those last 36 inches. On that day our will, desire, growth, and fight were all with him. On that day, it wasn't enough. He went down short of the goal line. Immediately the referees blew the whistle signaling the end of the game and they ran off the field to avoid any retaliation. As they hurried to get off the field, a sea of Howard fans were coming the opposite way to storm the field in celebration.

We lost and it hurt. Initially I dwelled on how Lewis didn't have his eyes up to see me. All he had to do was look up but, what happened, happened. His heart and effort were in the right place. If we say we had his back at the beginning of the day, then we should have his back at the end of it too. If I say, "I am my brother's keeper", that means I support the decisions and actions of my brothers when they have positive intentions for the greater good of the team. Win or lose, we do it together.

The only good thing about long bus rides after a loss, is no one is talking for 8-10 hours. Each individual has the space to process what just happened and how they feel about it. By the time we made it back home in the early hours of the next morning, stepping off the bus is like stepping out of yesterday. You literally step into a new day, a new week, and a new opportunity, with experience and reflection in hand.

"When something good happens, keep playing, when something bad happens keep playing. No matter what happens we stand together!"

The vision of raising the trophy and leaving a legacy of restoring the pride of A&T, never left my mind. It never left my heart. I felt like we had the right mindset, the right focus, and the right intent to will ourselves back on track. For some reason we were not able to right the ship. We lifted the weights, ran the sprints, practiced hard, studied long, and believed. In life you win with work, scheme, consistency, heart, endurance, and experience. The pieces of the puzzle we lacked were endurance and experience, both only obtained with time.

Maybe you have heard of Bill Gates or maybe Mark Zuckerberg. Both of these guys are technology giants. They weren't always that way. These men are outliers, but it's not because they were born the greatest programmers and businessman of their respective times. They are the greatest programmers and businessman of their respective times because of their reckless endurance. It allowed them to gain the experience which allowed them to excel. Their endurance to show up day after day, gaining experience after experience from their failures and successes, is what made them the greatest programmers. Then they used the experience of being consistent in the process in their development to become great businessmen. It transcended them into the sustaining billionaires they are today.

There is a difference between these two giants and most people. There came a day when it got hard, or something else tried to get in the way. Bill and Mark did not let anything sidetrack their focus. If they ran into adversity, they took it home, stayed up all night and showed back up early the next day. They confronted it. They spent the time and energy to figure it out.

Every day, every occurrence, and every play is a building block that stacks on top of the one before. It made us wiser, sharper, and more efficient. This is how compound interest works. Investing consistently allows your money and your abilities to build. It multiplies upon itself. Go look at a graph of compound interest. It doesn't say it, but it also represents the graph of success. Keep investing. Keep putting in the time and effort. Over time you will begin to reap the exponential profit.

Though we were giving it all we had, the experience gained from the consistency over time was something we could not magically inherit overnight. We were still a young team and our lack of experience opened holes in our armor as we went deeper into the fold. The way we lost to Howard exposed a few of those holes that we were diligently trying to fill.

One break in the yarn can be the start of ruining the most beautifully woven quilt. We began to unravel. As a leader I tried to put the load on my shoulders, but we lost the next three games to Norfolk State, Florida A&M, and South Carolina State. During this stretch I averaged 147 yards per game, but in case you forgot football is the ultimate team game. Averaging a ton of stats does not equate to wins or championships.

So many young athletes get caught up in stats and numbers. They are missing out on the greater concepts in the development of the team and the development of the people. The saying "You're only as good as your weakest link" is more correct than a calculator. If you are a great player, go the extra step by helping the guys next to you, below you, and above you. They may improve in the here and now, but you are also honing skills that will supply exponential profits for years to come. You win on both ends.

Yes, you need to stand out but, imagine this, it's 4th and 15 with no timeouts in the 4th quarter, and injuries have plagued the team. When it really comes down to it, who are you going to be looking at in the huddle to do their job? That third string Left Tackle, who is seeing his first action of the year, going up against the best defensive end in the league. If he doesn't hold that block, the quarterback won't have a chance to read the defense and deliver a strike to extend the game, extend the season, to extend the legacy. Good teams are formed from the top - down, but they are built for success from the bottom – up.

CHAPTER 48 - IT CAN'T END LIKE THIS

After losing four in a row, we were mathematically out of contention for the MEAC title we had fantasized about 4 months prior. Our dreams were gone, but had one more opponent, those dirty buzzards from down the road, North Carolina Central University. No matter where either of us were in the standings, the rivalry always made this game a big game.

This would be the last time I would suit up in a North Carolina A&T State University uniform. My heart was heavy, but my mind was full. I had watched four senior classes before me walk off the field from their last game with their heads bowed in defeat. The thought of that being my fate terrified me. Terrified me to do whatever it took not to suffer the fate my predecessors experienced.

This day signified a few opportunities for me individually to put my uncle's name amongst the Aggie immortals. It was an opportunity to become the first receiver to surpass 1,000 yards in a season, in school history. I had the opportunity to break the single season reception record and the opportunity to leave as the school's leader in career receptions. I was also in prime position to lead the team in receptions for the fourth consecutive season, a feat that had never been done. But, most importantly we had the opportunity to walk off the field winners solidifying the foundation of change we set out to build. This was an opportunity for the senior class of 2011 to put our final stamp on our legacy as North Carolina A&T State University student athletes. I was lacing up my cleats perhaps for the last time in my life, preparing to walk into my dreams. But all it takes is a split second for all your future opportunities and dreams to be erased. That is why we have to give all we have today, right now.

"SET HUT!" "Three steps attacking his leverage."

"Plant hard and explode inside."

"Snap your head around. See the ball,"

"Strong hands,"

"Good catch."

That was how a slant was supposed to play out. If you watched the film, it seemed like I went through exactly that process. In the moment, on the field, it went "SET HUT " ... "Rickey, how did I get the ball?" My teammate was standing over me attempting to help me up. A split second ago I was standing on the line, the next I was laying on my side with the ball in my hand with no clue how I got there.

"How did I get the ball?" I asked Rickey again.

When he heard this a second time he turned to our sideline and yelled "TRAINER!" He knew something was wrong with me, but I told him to chill. I knew what it might mean. Head injuries are a monumental issue in football. Part of the problem is the nature of the game. Part of the problem is the equipment that we wear is not ultimately sophisticated enough for the car crashes we find ourselves in week in and week out. The other part is the players. Between pride, ego, love of the game, stupidity, lack of self-care, or chasing a dream we try to hide and ignore symptoms of a concussion. All, so we can go back out there and potentially do it again.

As I came off to the sideline, I took my time, trying my best not to stumble. By the time I reached the trainers I had begun to gain my bearings. When the trainers took me through the concussion protocol, which consisted of questions about where you were, what you were doing, why you were there, who you were, what was the score, and what day it was. They checked my balance, my strength, my speech, and my eye focus. All of this is done to confirm you were of sound mind and body to go back in the game. I had been through this before and in the state I was in, I'm sorry to say I knew how to work the system. I spoke slowly and calmly, all the while thinking of what the day after Friday was. We play football on "Saturday!"

The trainers did their job. Asked every question, checked my equilibrium, checked my memory, and coordination. I exhibited all the capabilities to go back in the game, but for the second time in my career I ran on the field unsure if I should really be out there. This could be the last time I ever lined up to play the game that pulled the best out of me. Nothing was keeping me out of this game.

I didn't have much time to think about how I was feeling because as soon as I got back on the field, Lewis hit me on another slant. As soon as I touched the ball, everything was all good. Whether it was the magic of football or the power of passion, I was good to go.

From then on Lewis hit me early and often.

In the second quarter, Lewis called my favorite route, a dig. I counted the catch before we even snapped the ball. I did not realize what this play would mean though. As I came out of my break Lewis put it on me perfectly. I looked it all the way in and snagged it. Instead of running through the ball, for some reason I put the brakes on and changed directions. The corner who was covering me must not have expected this. How could he? I didn't even expect it. All I saw ahead of me was the green grass of the end zone, the cheerleaders who were already celebrating, and the stands behind them celebrating my every step. Oddly, in the midst

319

of this boisterous scene the volume of the world disappeared.

As I got closer and closer to the goal line a huge smile showed bright through the bars of my face mask. My journey to the goal line was not just the 37 yards I traveled on this particular play. It started before I was even allowed to cross the white lines onto the field. It started walking down to the park with my Aunt Mae watching all the other kids in pads playing the sport I was instinctively drawn to. From standing on the other side of the fence watching other people play, to being the one everyone in a packed stadium was watching, so much had happened on my journey. Mental battles, physical growth, injuries, kicking, fighting, screaming, running, learning, and EVOLVING!

As I crossed the threshold of the end zone, it was as if someone grabbed the remote and turned the volume up. A thunderous roar of celebration flooded my ears. As I always did, I turned back to celebrate with my teammates. I was late to my own party. Half the team had cleared the bench and was running toward the end zone to meet me. The love I felt from my brothers in that moment made every moment it took to get to this point in life worth it to go through ten times over. The team took a 15-yard penalty for excessive celebration to celebrate me.

When we finally made our way to the sideline, the announcer came over the loudspeaker: "With that catch and run, Wallace Miles becomes the first A&T player with over 1,000 receiving yards in a single season. He also broke the record for most receptions by an A&T player in a season." When I heard this the joy I felt went away and was replaced with an immense feeling of pride.

Three years prior I was walking down the streets of Baltimore, MD with my dad visualizing this day. The dream of this day was birthed on the same streets the dreams of my name sake was taken away. I could never have seen the journey to this place, but I believed there was a way to the dream I now stood in.

I thought of everything it took to get to this point, but also everyone it took to get this point. In all the chaos I looked up to the stands where my family was sitting. Twenty people had again interrupted their lives for a day to travel from near and far to support me in this moment. To show my respect to these amazing people I stood on the bench and raised my right fist to the sky in reverence of their love and support. I think they got the message because, just as they did when I graduated high school, they filled the sky with their fists as a symbol of our oneness, with my parent's and my sister's hands lifted above them all.

I wouldn't have had the fortitude to stay on this path this long without the support of the blood that raised me. That fist was raised to everyone in the stands that day, but also to all those who could not be there but had nurtured my growth. This is who you do it for. Those who gave some of their life force and put it into you. The ultimate respect to them is to go and do something positive with their investment.

Coach Harper, who was always focused on getting the win, wasn't too happy about the penalty, but I could tell he was proud of the moment. We still had a football game to win, which we did. Our senior class was the first class to walk off the field after their last game as Aggies victorious in almost a decade.

As I took the walk back to the locker room for the last time, I tried to take in as much of the moment as I could. The stands, the grass, the goal post, the sidelines, the logo, and the Aggie statue. As I crossed into the end zone for the last time, something came over me. A weight of emotion pulled the tears I was determined to hold back out of my eyes and down my cheeks. One drop leaked out and a river followed.

The memory of walking onto this field as a walk-on kicker and the struggle to become who I knew I could be as I walked off, was overwhelming. The point of this book is to let you, the reader, know that whatever direction you feel pulling at your heart no matter what you are being told or pushed into, find the moment to choose your path. Take control of your life and change your stars. Take a knee, take a breath, and change your cleats. Your passion will pull and fulfill you further than you could have ever seen. You have to make the shift because your life is and will always only be yours. Once you commit to you, with work, the universe will conspire to see you into opportunities and through challenges. It will allow you to digest the knowledge, love, and the growth necessary for you to become who you were meant to be.

OVERTIME

CHAPTER 49 - CATCH'M BOTH

I hope you didn't think this was over. When you aren't a top-rated prospect, and millions of dollars aren't promised to you, there is a mental limbo you have to transition through. This place evaluates all possible outcomes.

Questions that need answers fill your mind. Will I ever play again? What do I need to do next? Can I make it on the next level? What if I don't make it? Doubt and insecurity begin swirling within you, while your exterior has to remain calm and confident. You have to go through this place because there is no place for "I don't know" or "I'm not sure" moving forward on this journey. It's going to leave you fragile. You have to go through this place, to prepare your mind for the injuries, the riches, the failure, and triumph, whatever is thrown at you. Understand how much work is going to be required and how draining the life could be. Understand how it could change the trajectory of your entire family. Is it worth it?

Once you go through this mental space you will have to arrive at a decision. A decision that you have broken down, evaluated, visualized, and internalized. A decision that will alter the direction, but not necessarily the trajectory of your life. You have to reach the point of commitment.

There is no shame in stepping away from the game having learned so many of life's lessons. There is nothing wrong with taking all you have become and starting a career outside of that thing that has walked with you for so long. That thing you have clung tight too thus far along the way.

My decision after a long deliberation was that I wasn't ready to let it go. After my eligibility was up, there was no guarantee I was going to be selected to play again. How was I going to keep it going? Milt had given me the answer to that question years before. The decision was made, now I had to "Find a Way!"

Many of my draft eligible counterparts were leaving school to go focus exclusively on training and getting ready for whatever opportunity showed itself to them. Though I haven't dwelled on the importance of school too deeply, it still was a massive priority in my life. I had put 4 ½ years toward attaining my Electrical Engineering degree. I was all in on my dream to go to the NFL, but I was taught at a young age to see whatever you start to the end. If I was going to go after the NFL and I had to finish school.

I once had a coach that had two quarterbacks throw two balls to me at the same time while I was running a route. I dropped both of them. I asked him what I was supposed to do. His simple response was "Catch them both!"

JUGGLING ACT

One day I happened to be watching a special on Bengals receiver, AJ Green. They went through his life and how he became the perennial Pro-Bowler you see today. Yes, he is tall. Yes, he is fast but there is something that has always set AJ Green apart. Remember what Milt said you catch the ball with. "Your eyes!" AJ learned how to juggle in elementary school. This juvenile ability might have seemed to be just something fun to do for a ten year old, but it became one of his greatest assets. It's the reason he is able to routinely make the toughest catches. From a young age he had trained his eyes to track the trajectory of an object and put himself in position to receive it.

They showed a video of him in elementary school and then flashed forward to the present. He was still juggling to train his eyes. After watching this I did the only thing that logically made sense. I drove to the dollar store, bought 3 tennis balls, and came back to my room. From there I proceeded to teach myself how to juggle. For about a week it was more like, how many different ways can you drop a tennis ball, but one day I finally got two full cycles, and then I got 5. Two weeks in and I was juggling. I was training my eyes like AJ, but I was also training my eyes to catch more than one goal. "Catch them both!"

While being aware of the other goals in your peripheral, pick one ball, analyze, and develop Plan 1A to catch it. Then focus on the second, analyzing and developing Plan 1B, while keeping Plan 1A in your peripheral. Ultimately to catch both balls, you will find yourself in a compromise between both plans, let's call it Plan 1C. Plan 1C considers the effort, positioning, focus, and technique of both Plan 1A and Plan 1B. To catch both balls, we have to remove all other distractions by focusing on executing the plan that puts you in position to catch 1A and 1B. When it's catching two balls, all of this happens in seconds. When planning to achieve two goals, you may have more time, but time is always fleeting. We must analyze, plan, and execute with a sense of urgency.

PLAN 1A

Now that my goals were defined, I had two milestones ahead of me. Graduation and my pro day. Pro day is normally the last opportunity for college athletes to present their physical abilities to NFL teams. It is the in person interview to support the film resume you have established during your playing career. For a young player from a small school this is a crucial opportunity. When you watch the big schools' pro day, you will see all 32 teams represented to test the abilities of that school's prospects. When you are at a small school you may have been lucky to have had two teams represented. This year Coach Prince told us that seven teams would have representatives to come see us.

The stage was set. I knew where one ball was going to land. Now how was I going to be in that place, ready? Every question has an answer, and every problem has a solution. I knew how to play receiver, but I had never been the fastest, jumped the highest, or been the strongest. Our pro-day was only going to test our physical attributes. I needed someone to teach and train me to put my best foot forward.

What do you do when you don't know? "Find a way." I remembered hearing that Chris Kennedy, one of my former teammates, was working at a place called Victorious Place. I got in contact with Chris, and he gave me the rundown of the facility. I found out that Victor Hope, the Super Bowl winning receiver with the Green Bay Packers, was the owner. Chris gave me the phone number of the head sports and performance trainer, a guy named Rodney. I called him and expressed to him that I wanted to train with him, but I didn't have much money. He told me to come to a workout at 6pm the next day.

I showed up the next day, at 5:30. I remembered the last time I showed up to a training session late with Milt, so I didn't want to take a chance. Chris introduced me to Rodney. Rodney told me to hop in line with his crew of young kids who were about to begin their workout. I couldn't believe he wanted me to get in line with a bunch of high school boys and girls. I was trying to go to the NFL, I couldn't be working out with these kids.

By the time we finished that day, it didn't matter if I was in a group of infants or the best athletes on the planet. Rodney had a way of making you compete and work on your level. The kids were a bonus because you could feel the pure joy of just being out there. As what you are chasing becomes a business, some of the fun can be lost in the muck. These kids helped me retain the joy.

After the workout, I stayed behind with Rodney to talk. He was excited about the effort, energy, and fun I showed during the workout. I think this had an effect on what he said before I left. "Can you do $100 a month?" My eyes widened and I'm sure my mouth dropped. I had met trainers that charged $100 a session. This was a blessing in plain sight. Rodney then put a cherry on top. He told me that he had a crew of professional athletes and guys that were training for their NFL opportunities who trained earlier in the day. When you show you want something, people will appear in your life to help you. "When you show", not when you "say", that's when they will come!

It's instinctive for people to want to help people. No one wants to give their time and energy to someone who seems disinterested. At the end of the day, the equation of life is the $L = (E*I*E)^T$ (energy x interest x efficiency you put in)^ (the time you have). In a sense when someone gives their time to you, they in essence give you a major piece of their life. No one will want to waste their life. When you see someone giving you their life, treat it as if it were that precious.

I saw what Rodney was giving to my life. Although I had only just met him, I wanted him to see that I appreciated him offering some of his life and experience to me. I did that by driving the 30 minutes there and back twice a day 4 times a week for 2-hour sessions. I would work out with the pros at 10AM and then again with the younger crew at 6PM. I showed my appreciation by giving max effort in everything he asked me to do and bringing a positive attitude every day, no matter what was going on.

PLAN 1B

Now that Plan 1A was set, I still needed to graduate. Most of my classmates would go to class for 4 hours a day and have the rest of the day to relax, study, hang out, and have fun. For what I was trying to accomplish, I did not have the luxury to relax and hang out. I knew missing class was not an option. I had to continue to go to class to gain the information. I also needed to build rapport with my teachers and classmates because I recognized I needed help.

As an experienced student, I knew that just sitting in class was not going to cut it when it came to grasping and passing these classes. I was going to have to put in time completing assignments and studying. I just didn't know when. As I looked at the landscape of my classes, there was a nucleus of the same students. Many of these students I could call friends and some I had just met. In either case I asked if they were studying after school, when, and where? From my surveys I found a group that would conduct evening sessions. They normally gathered around 7pm at an apartment off campus and would go at it often until after midnight.

This crew knew what I was trying to accomplish. They knew all I was doing to accomplish my goal. They also knew I wanted to graduate and was willing to show up and work. I wasn't as advanced as these guys, but because they felt my genuine effort, they would go over assignments they had already completed with me. They would work to break down the methods we were learning so I could grasp them. They would stop their own work to answer questions I had. These were genuinely good people but "when you show you want to, they will come!" I can credit this group of people, this group of friends with helping me catch Plan 1B.

PLAN 1C

Eventually I found a rhythm. I would wake up at 6am to start the day. Go to class, then to Victorious at 10am, and back to class by 12:30pm. When I finished up in class, I would head back to Victorious at 6pm. I would finish up there around 8pm and head to the study group funky and all. We would study until we all gave in to the exhaustion then wake up and do it all over again. If that wasn't enough, some Friday nights or Saturday mornings, I would travel to Atlanta to work with Milt over the weekend to be back in Greensboro by Monday morning. This was the only plan I could develop that I believed would allow me to "Catch them both". I could get to the NFL and walk across the stage to grab hold of my diploma. There wasn't time to hang out. There wasn't time to relax.

At some point in your journey to get over the hump, to attain something special, you will have to go underground. You will have to go to a mental place where the only thing on the agenda is what it takes to succeed.

Most people won't have the vision or passion that you have in this moment of life. Your life and your goals will always be unique to you. They won't understand that achieving your goal is time sensitive. Unintentionally they will try to lead you off your path. Do you want it bad enough to pass on the party? Do you want it bad enough to pass on the young lady that wants you to miss a workout or a class to have a little fun? How bad do you want it? You don't have to tell anyone the answer to this. Your sacrifice and decision making will tell you everything you need to know.

CHAPTER 50 - PATH TO THE DRAFT

Guys from small schools have this stigma. Since they have not competed on the highest level of college football, their competition level doesn't compare to guys from big schools. This inserted itself along with the other doubt that I constantly battled with. Working with Rodney proved to be the right move for what I was trying to do. Competing with guys that had been where I was trying to go, propelled me physically. It also helped improve my confidence for what I was trying to accomplish.

As the weeks went on, I began to see improvement in my technique, my strength, endurance, speed, and explosiveness. The big test for a receiver is his 40 yard dash. I told you I had never been the fastest and for some reason I could not seem to lower my 40 time. I consistently ran in the mid to high 4.6's, which is not terrible, but it would not garner the attention I was working to spark. Going into my pro day I was nervous to put that time in front of the scouts.

The day of our pro day, my dad came up. He brought with him the support of my entire family. We had a calming breakfast. As nervous as I was, he assured me that throughout my entire life I had been preparing for what was before me. He assured me that the success came in the preparation. I knew I had prepared, and it was time to show. My mother, who was unable to be there, sent me a text with the mantra she had spoken into me throughout my entire life. "Show up and show out!" Reading those words boiled a focused intensity up through me. We finished our breakfast and headed over to the field house where everyone was starting to congregate.

When all the scouts arrived, Coach Prince called us all up and handed it over to the scout from the Titans. They took all of our measurables, height, weight, hand size, vertical reach, and body fat. After we got all the formalities out of the way it was time to get to work. As much as I wanted to enjoy the process, in a blink of an eye it was over. I went into a zone that I had rarely felt. My body was moving on its own. I came out on the other side of my pro day proud of what I put on my resume. Vertical jump 35.5", 12 reps at 225 pounds, 6.87 L Drill, and 4.1 shuttle. I was even proud of my 40 yard dash, even though it wasn't eye popping at a 4.6, it was mine and I earned it. I worked for it. It wasn't the event of my pro day that my pride resided. It was the journey to it. If we establish our goals, analyze the circumstances, put a plan together, and execute, growth along with confidence will emerge from the process.

When it was all over and I had come back to earth, something I did caught the attention of two scouts. Remember it only takes 1 team to like you. The Steelers and Falcons both pulled me aside. They expressed enthusiasm with my workout. They both liked the way I moved through the drills, something I had never thought about. They told me I was fluid, that I had good hips, and that I had good knee bend and explosiveness in and out of my breaks. They both mentioned that they wished my 40 time was better, but they were pleased with the overall performance. The event that I spent 8 weeks preparing for was over. The moment was good, but the journey was so much more.

ALL A MAN CAN ASK FOR IS A CHANCE

It seemed like life has these cycles. After I completed my pro day and all my requirements moving toward graduation, I still had no real solid plan for what I would do when I left school. I would have an Electrical Engineering degree in hand and an illustrious football career in my past with nowhere to go. I was afraid. I believed that fear was part of the reason I kept working like there was a tomorrow. I kept working like I knew they would call me.

Thursday April 26, 2012, The NFL Draft officially opens, with the Indianapolis Colts taking Andrew Luck number 1 overall. For the next 3 days I watched and listened to 253 names called. None of them being mine. As the last player, Chandler Harnish, was called my head dropped. The doubt began to swirl. In order to avoid feeling the rejection from the game I loved, I got up and went to the gym. It was the only thing I knew to do to relieve the building tension on my head. Not getting drafted was not the biggest surprise to me, but I did think maybe someone would want to sign me as a priority free agent. Nope, no contact of any kind. Wandering around the gym with my headphones blasting, I was lost again!

The next day I woke up and went to class. I then went to Victorious Park, trained, came back, and finished up class, then went back to Victorious. My mindset was that I was just going to continue to work because I believed the journey wasn't over. They had to call me. They had to have seen the potential.

Something I had maintained in the shadows, but had an illuminating light, was prayer. I prayed for an opportunity to continue my career. I prayed that this young man who was just catching his stride after years of hard work, had earned a chance to show that he could compete at the highest level. If it didn't work out, I would be cool knowing that I had a chance and wasn't good enough at the time. I prayed while I was at stop lights. I prayed while I was in the cafeteria when I was supposed to be praying for my food. I prayed as I walked across campus. My dream was always on my mind and I knew whose hands it was really in.

By the third day I was pretty numb to my daily activities. I was losing expression and losing enthusiasm. I was pretty much on auto pilot. All I could think of was, be ready when the phone rings. I was in the gym one morning, lifting on my own, with my music blasting and in my own zone. Out of nowhere my music goes off, which is normally a sign there is an incoming call. I looked down and grabbed my phone. I did not recognize the number shown, but underneath the number it said, Allen Park, Michigan. "Couldn't be!"

"Hello!"

"Yes, may I speak to Wallace Miles?" the voice on the other end asked.

"This is he." I responded.

He introduced himself as Cedric Saunders, Vice President of Player Personnel for the Detroit Lions. My heart began pounding. My voice began to shake. I was talking to a representative of my favorite NFL organization. I thought "He is about to offer me a contract. "I'm going to be a Detroit Lion" talk about dreams coming true. That's not what came next.

"I just wanted to see if you would be interested in coming to our rookie minicamp, we might have an opening for you but I'm not sure yet. If we do, I'll call you back." Mr. Saunders said.

"Yes sir I'm looking forward to your call."

I hung up, with a chance that I might have a chance. That was great news to me.

I finished my workout and decided to take a nap. I normally can't sleep during the day, but I think my never ending schedule had caught up to me. Within minutes I was out cold. I don't know how long I was out, but I was awakened by the phone ringing in my ear. My heart started jumping out of my chest as it was the same Michigan number that had called me earlier. I didn't want him to hear the voice of someone who was waking up at 10:30 in the morning. So, I practiced saying "Hello" a couple times. Once I felt I got it right I picked up and said

"Hello!"

"Yes Wallace, we do have an opportunity for you."

He asked if I wanted to accept this chance. Of course, I agreed.

He told me that I wasn't going to be signing a contract. This was just an opportunity to try out at rookie minicamp. He told me someone would be contacting me about my travel arrangements, and I said, "Thank you!" I had a chance to go to my favorite team to earn a spot. I couldn't be happier. I began to reflect on my auspicious start at A&T. Being given an opportunity to walk on as the last man on the roster. "I've been here before!"

I received an email with a flight itinerary, as well as the duration of the camp. The email stated I was to leave at 6:00 am, May 10, 2011 and would return May 13 at 5:15pm. Two things immediately stuck out to me. One of the biggest accomplishments of my life to date was already scheduled for May 12th. It was the day I was to walk across the stage for my graduation from college. All the hard work, late nights, emotional highs, and lows, culminated in the symbol of completion, the diploma. Walking across the stage accepting your diploma from the Chancellor, and basking in the glory of the journey, is a moment of a lifetime.

As I began to think about the conflict, I concluded that graduation day was just a symbol. I technically did not have to be there to graduate. This realization solidified the answer to the decision I had to make, but I had to break the news to my parents. They took it as a great opportunity. My mother was a little hurt by my decision because graduation is really for her, but as she has my entire life, she supported whatever I wanted to do. Even missing my own college graduation.

The second thing that came to my attention in that email was the return date. The issue wasn't the date, May 13th. The fact that there was a return date at all is what bothered me. I was going up there with the intentions of not coming back. To me that date said we aren't expecting much from you. I was probably looking for any added motivation from anywhere because, motivation is everywhere. Having the mindset of not coming back I packed all my stuff up so my parents could come up and get all my stuff while I was gone.

I told my close friends and my teammates about the news. I thought I was excited about the news, but they were ecstatic. It was so rare that anyone from A&T even got a chance with a professional team, let alone in the NFL. In my time at A&T only one player had ever gotten a workout with an NFL team and that was 3 years after he left A&T. The idea of me getting invited to rookie minicamp, even unsigned was a big deal.

As the departure date got closer, my excitement and anticipation began to escalate. I had thoughts of all the possibilities. Lining up next to the great receiver Andre

Jackson, meeting Barry Sanders, even donning the silver helmet with the charging lion, all seemed surreal to me. As a child I grew up a Lions fan because I loved Barry Sanders. He was my childhood sports idol. Not Michael Jordan. Not Jerry Rice. Not Michael Johnson, but quiet, electrifying Barry Sanders. I wanted to go to Westlake High school because I thought it would be my only chance to be a Lion. As fate had it, I was getting a chance to do it again. In my mind it was going to be a storybook ending when it was all said and done.

CHAPTER 51 - THE WALK-ON REAPPEARS

Six o'clock in the morning on May 10th, 2011, I was taking off to my dreams. When I landed in Detroit, I found a guy holding a sign with my name on it with the Lions logo. Every step made the situation more real. He packed my bags in a car and drove me to Allen Park, Michigan, where the lions training facility is located. As we pulled in, my heart started doing the thumping thing again. Anticipation began flowing through my body. Someone was there to meet me at the front of this big blue building. I was introduced to the front desk security attendant, then I was taken back to the locker room.

The facilities were nothing like I had ever seen. The lockers were wood finished with leather cushioned seats. Every locker had its own stool in front with the players name and number. Everything looked official, except for these caged portable lockers in the middle of the room where of course I happened to see my name taped. I didn't care because I was in the Detroit Lions locker room. My guide for the time being showed me the weight room, training room, pool areas, and the indoor field. Then he asked me if I wanted to meet the receivers. "I'm about to meet Andre Jackson" is what I thought. I said "Sure!" He led me down the hallway to the receiver room. They were in the middle of watching a film when I walked in.

Coach Marcus Middleton, the receivers coach, had me stand front and center and introduce myself. I stood in front of Calvin Johnson, Titus Young, Stefan Logan, Terrance Tolliver, Nate Burleson, and Nate Hughes, and said "My name is Wallace Miles, wide receiver from Atlanta, Ga. and I attended North Carolina Agricultural and Technical State University."

They allowed me to sit in on their meeting watching film from the previous season. It was pretty relaxed. A few jokes were cracked, but everyone seemed to have a professional focus. Very much unlike the meetings back at school where guys didn't always behave with a purpose. This felt like the place for me.

After Coach Middleton let us out of the meeting, I was starstruck when Calvin Johnson, who stood 6'5, 240 lbs., approached me. He is really a gentle giant off the field. He was raised in the Atlanta area also, so we had an immediate rapport. He began talking about home. His older sister actually went to my high school, so he said he was at Westlake a lot growing up. I was sitting here talking with a guy who I tried to emulate. We walked and talked for about five minutes after the meeting, just kicking it. The last thing he told me before we went our separate ways was "I hope to see you Monday bro, just make plays!" When he said that, reality hit me again. I wasn't guaranteed to be there past rookie minicamp. The next battle in my life was on the brink of commencing.

After talking with Calvin, I was taken to the hotel where I just dropped all my stuff and called my parents. They and my sister, Claudia have always been the governing board to my fan club. Talking with them reinforced the positive energy within me and fought off the doubt that always hovered in the shadows. I was ready to attack. My mother constantly reminded me that I still had an electrical engineering degree, and everything would be ok either way. I honestly didn't want to hear any of that, but what she was trying to do was relieve my mind of the self-imposed weight. She wanted me to play free. She wanted me to "show up and show out". Pops gave me some things to think about and he ended with what had become one of his catchphrases, "Catch the ball boy!"

My roommate came in while I was talking to my folks. He was a tall lanky guy, from the University of Massachusetts. When you are in the process of earning a position on a team, whether in college or in the pros you will probably encounter the roommate situation. In these situations, you tend to spend a lot of time getting to know a person, even though your goal is to beat them out and possibly send them home. Everyone has their own story to get to the place you are. They are the culmination of that story. Though you are there to take the position you both are aiming for, connecting with people who have experienced the world from a completely different perspective is one of the greatest opportunities there is. We can study, practice, and do, all day long. The true growth in our humanity is fertilized in our connectivity to the other human beings around us.

There was one other mission I had to accomplish that night. In all the hoopla of this opportunity, I had to finish my final paper for my senior project. I had no computer so, I sat in my bed and in the Notes app on my phone, I finished my paper. Yes, I wrote my last paper to graduate college in a hotel bed on my phone.

I emailed my work to one of my most trusted friends at A&T, Marcell. He put it in a word document, spell and grammar checked it, then turned it in the next morning for me. I am forever grateful for the true friends that helped me succeed on the field, but just as importantly in the classroom. Brotherhoods are forged in the struggle. The struggle of football and class created some eternal bonds with some amazing people. With this last act of friendship mixed with procrastination I was officially a college graduate.

The next morning, we took the shuttle to the facility to attend the first team meeting. This meeting consisted of draft picks, priority free agents, and us tryout guys. Head Coach, Tim Gardner, headed up the meeting and he gave it to us straight.

"Some of you guys are going home in three days. This is the opportunity to show you deserve to stay."

The draft picks were pretty much safe, while the free agent signees had to prove a little bit more, while the tryout guys had to shine bright in order to see tomorrow. We had to stand out among all the guys the Lions had already invested in. "I've been here before!" again went through my mind.

We separated into offensive and defensive meeting rooms to begin installing plays. The play calling had a lot more verbiage than we did in college where there was a formation, a protection, and a play. Though I knew the language of football, the dialect of the NFL was tough to comprehend, at first.

After we met for about an hour and a half, we were set for our first practice. The rookie receivers consisted of

Patrick Edwards, a guy out of Houston who had 20 touchdowns his last year. Troy Burrell, a guy who probably should have won the Harlon Hill Trophy, for best player in the country at the Division II level. Then there was Donald Benton, a cerebral receiver from Oregon State. My roommate Greg Walton, out of Massachusetts, myself, and last but not least the NCAA's career leader in receptions at the time, Ryan Broyles from Oklahoma. Life is funny sometimes. Eight months before I was watching Ryan's stat line on every bus ride hoping to keep pace with him week in and week out. I knew when it came to making it to the NFL, I wouldn't just be compared to other FCS players. I would have to compete with the best and Ryan was the best!

At the time of minicamp, he was still recovering from an ACL injury. He was not healthy enough to practice, so he watched the rest of us. Needless to say, we had a lot of collegiate talent in the rookie receiver group. I was excited to see what I could take from each of them to add to my game, but that hovering doubt made its presence known. "With so much talent, how am I going to stand out?" Greg and I were the only tryout guys in the group. Everyone else had already been signed to contracts.

Practice began and Coach Marcus Middleton displayed energy I had never seen out of a coach on any level. We fed off of it, creating the most intense individual period I had ever experienced. By the time it was time to catch some balls from the quarterbacks, we were all breathing heavy. No one wanted to show how bad they felt. We were all there to push our limits. The competition was on and poppin'.

By the time we got to one on one's against the DBs, we started to catch that second wind that Coach Middleton was trying to fish out of us. This was my first chance to go against what was considered NFL ready talent. The guy I most wanted to go against was Roy Hearn, the third round draft pick out of LSU. I had read up on him as I had done on all the DB's in camp. He was fast, pretty good at reading routes, patient and quick at breaking on the ball. I wanted a chance at him, just like I had wanted a shot at AD in high school. I got exactly what I was asking for. He was what the scouts said he was, but I wasn't what they thought I was. Every time I went against him, we got better. He covered me then I beat him. In every period of practice, I wanted to line up against what was supposed to be their best in camp.

Practice #1 ended ok. We had to go to weight training and meetings later that day. We installed more plays and watched the film from practice. Coach Middleton was a hard critic. He was a huge stickler of the little things. No false steps, your leverage aiming point, pumping your arms, getting your head around, being quick out of your break.

"Where were your eyes while you were running your route? Did you take your eyes to the ball all the way through the catch? Did you catch it with your hands?"

He would go through all these details on every route on the screen. It began to irritate me, but I figured this is another difference between the MEAC and the NFL. I learned quickly to eat my words and take my coaching. Even if it took 15 minutes to get through one play.

In the midst of all the coaching that evening, Coach Middleton unleashed a phrase that has resonated in every corner of my life ever since. "Stay ready so you never have to get ready!" It's blunt and means exactly what it says. If you always stay ready for whatever opportunity you are looking for, when it comes you will be ready to take full advantage. If you have to take time to get ready when that time arrives, you're already too late.

CHAPTER 52 - THE BEGINNING AT THE END

Day two began the same as day one, with a team meeting followed by an offensive meeting. There we reviewed what was installed the day before and added more. Then it was time to go at it again. In the receiver group, it felt like pure competition. We were all trying to make the next play. Coach Middleton was continually on us about the minor details, literally yelling at us as we ran a route or through a drill. Even though we were competing to earn one of the limited spots, I never felt any malice in the group. It felt pure. We supported each other and celebrated with each other as we tried to beat each other.

I was excited about practice, mainly because I wanted another chance at Roy. I was learning him as he was learning me, so it was a great competition. I never really said anything when I beat him, but as a defensive back, he was much more talkative when he made a play. What do you expect? He did come up to me once. "Bro, what school did you come from?" I told him A&T, and of course, he didn't know what or where that was, but he followed up with, "Bro, you cold!" We talked a little more, and he couldn't believe I was just a tryout player. Sound familiar? Unknowingly he was clearing up the doubt of whether or not I could compete on this level. Our third-round pick projected starting Nickelback was giving me props after two practices.

We both were just trying to make this team, but when you are in the grind, in the midst of competition, you really just want to be your best on each rep. What is deeper than beating an outside force is overcoming yourself **every play**. Overcoming the doubt, overcoming old habits, overcoming your feelings, and depositing all your efforts in this individual moment. This will build those dreams of making the team and supporting your family.

I once heard actor and music artist *Will Smith* telling the story of how his father had him and his younger brother build a wall for their storefront. He states that he looked at the <u>task</u> of building a wall as daunting and was doubtful they would complete it. In the process of building this wall that took an entire summer to build, he learned that the ultimate goal is always the process of depositing all his effort in laying each brick as perfectly as he could. When you look back at all the bricks you have laid, you will realize you have built a wall to stand the test of time. How do you think the Great Wall of China was built? Don't worry, I'll answer for you, "Brick by brick!" That's how we reach our dreams in life. We do so brick by brick. That philosophy is how I came from twelve catches in high school to be in a position to earn a spot with the team of my dreams. I did it rep by rep. I did it showing up day after day. "Life is a process not an event!" Lay your brick as perfectly as you can every day.

Day Three was the last chance I had to impress someone enough for them to want to keep me, and of course, my day started off poorly. I dropped a comeback route. This was it there was no tomorrow, what are you going to do? Coach Harper popped in my head, "When something bad happens..." I just kept playing. I just kept fighting. I bounced back and made a few plays—the biggest being on a 7 step post in stride for an 80 yards touchdown.

The last whistle blew. The signal that it was all over. All my opportunities to impress the Detroit Lions and become a member of the NFL were spent. Looking at my wall, I was proud of what I had built. Coach Gardner called us all up and thanked us all for the effort we had put forth over the past 3 days. Then for the final time we broke it down.

"HARD WORK ON THREE! ONE... TWO... THREE... HARD WORK!" As we huddled for the last time at rookie minicamp, I couldn't believe where I was. Standing on an NFL field, a place I had dreamed about. I was surrounded by 50 other guys who were standing in the midst of their version of the same dream. The ambiance intensified. Though we all worked so hard to get here, we all were approaching a pivotal point in our lives that was no longer in our control. Pride and joy came face to face with fear and doubt. It created a toiling of emotion within me. There was nothing more I could do but hope I was enough.

As we all started walking to the sidelines, heading to the locker room, my eyes jumped around to see how my peers were reacting to this moment. Some were stoic, seemingly unfazed by the moment. There were some joking and playing around. They were either oblivious to what was about to happen or confident in their position. There were those that were like me, conscious of the enormity of the situation with concern stamped all over their faces.

As I continued to scan my surroundings, my eyes came across a set of eyes that seemed to be looking right back at me. The doubt swirling within said: "He is looking past you." The owner of this set of eyes started walking toward me with a smile on his face. The doubt continued to whisper, "He's going to talk to someone else!" But as our paths reached a connecting point, he stopped right in front of me. The owner of that set of eyes was Chris Trotter, the General Manager of the Detroit Lions. He told me I had a good camp and that I showed a lot over the last three days. Overtaken by the moment, I managed to respond, "Thank you, I appreciate the opportunity" Then he told me something that almost broke me down on the spot. I never knew how impactful words could be or how much emotion they could trigger until this moment. Every second I had spent on a field practicing, watching film, in a gym lifting weights or in my bed dreaming a dream, had all brought me to this moment. Mr. Trotter said, "WE'RE GOING TO SIGN YOU!"

Looking him square in his eyes I searched for the breath to speak but, all of the conditioning in the world could not give me what it took for this moment. Eventually in all my searching I was able to muster, a calm "Thank you sir, I really appreciate the opportunity." All the life that had drained out of me only seconds before was now rushed back allowing me to feel the moment from the crown of my head down to the soles of my feet.

Walking off the field turned into a sprint to the locker room. I had to talk to my parents. I needed to talk to my parents. My phone was filled with text messages and missed phone calls from them. There were a lot of guys in the locker room that were packing up to head home. When I realized this, I felt it would be wrong to call and tell my folks the good news in front of them. I ran to the bathroom and got in the handicap stall. I called my dad, no answer. I called my mom, no answer! I called dad again, no answer. I started to call my mother again, but my phone rang. My dad was calling me back. When I answered the phone, he sounded very drowsy. My parents are those parents that wake up at 7 AM on weekends even when they have nothing to do. For him to sound like he was just waking up at 11 o'clock, was odd. I asked if he had gone to church.

"No, we stayed up all night because we were worried about you. We hadn't heard from you" he replied.

I abruptly told him "They are going to sign me!" and he let out a yell with excitement.

"Way to go Wallace. He's getting signed" he said to my mother as he celebrated.

In that moment, my mind shot back to my days at Westlake when I couldn't even get a rep at practice. I thought about my last game at Westlake that was supposed to be it. Fast forwarding to walking on to A&T's team and changing my cleats, the moment I chose "ME!" All the time I spent working out. So much of it alone on a hill or a field somewhere. As soon as my mother spoke on the phone, "Hey Wally J.", completely overwhelmed with my journey to this moment, I began to cry. They say, "There is no crying in football!" Well, there was today. I didn't try to hold these choking, snotty, tears back at all. I boo hoo sobbed on the floor of that stall with my parents on the phone.

I believed for so long that I wasn't supposed to be where I was. A change in mindset caused me to believe I could be here when no one else could see it. My infatuation with football started with Barry Sanders and the Detroit Lions. Now, I was here. My pops, hearing me crying, asked me was I ok? I managed to say "yes". He like no one else knew where I came from when it came to football. He started me in the back yard when I wasn't even allowed to play, running what he called "button hooks", the 1950 version of the curl route.

My mother got back on the phone with the same energy my dad had exhibited. I think she started to tear up, but she held it together. She told me how worried she was when I didn't answer the night before. She told me how much she loved me. She told me how much I deserved this. She told me she prayed for me all night.

I will never forget that moment. I will use that moment to pick me up in some of my toughest times for the rest of my life. That's what you have to do sometimes, reach back to your happiest, triumphant character defining moments to remind yourself that you have what it takes to overcome adverse circumstances. These are reminders that you can find happiness again and that the power of joy is in you.

Now on the flip side we must constantly reject the feelings of the negative memories we have experienced. See what I said. "Reject the negative feelings". Never forget the lessons that your failures teach you, but don't dwell in the feeling of failure. No matter who you are or what you do in this life you are going to meet adversity face to face. It will take everything you are and everything you have experienced to overcome it. Hold on to your experiences. Grow from them. Become from them. Occasionally you may need a jump start. Go back to that "WHY" you wrote down, and feel the power it generates. They won't understand your source as you continue to push. To be UNDERR8TED is to be more than they know.

I don't know you, but I believe in you. I pray that one day we can sit face to face, and we can show each other what no one else ever saw. Don't wait, choose you and go be great today!

EPILOGUE

The book you have just read is the story of a portion of my life. I hope you can take with you the lessons I had to learn through the journey of life. The lessons we learn in life are what widen our gaze and help us along this wild rollercoaster.

I truly believe that I am no better than you. We all will have our own stories. My story will not be your story, and your story will not be mine. Our lives are here for each other to grow from. Something you learn from my life may carry you forward. But on the flip side, one day, when we meet or maybe through email (changeyourcleats@gmail.com) I can learn something from your journey.

I will forever be grateful that you took the time to read my story. I pray you received value that will pay dividends for the rest of your life.

It's funny. It took me eight years to write my own story. But, in those eight years, though I had the same eyes I was born with the entire time, I see the world and my life very differently. Perspective shapes your reality. Your perspective is shaped by the knowledge you gain and the lessons you learn. Never stop working to learn more. You'll see your view of the same world will. More options will open themselves to you, and the more you learn, the more potential you have to earn.

Remember this, whatever success we achieve in this world will more than likely stand on the shoulder of thousands of failures. You will fail countless times. If you chose yourself and chose a path attached to your heart, the failures will just be teaching moments that invigorate you to step back to the plate.

I did go on to play for the Detroit Lions in the NFL. I then touched down in Canada, where I played for the Winnipeg Blue Bombers, Ottawa Red Blacks, Edmonton Eskimos, and Toronto Argonauts, winning a Grey Cup, the CFL Super Bowl, with the Eskimos. All that is a story for another day, but the only reason I was able to experience those opportunities is because I decided to unrelentingly chase what I believed was for me. Choose you, and become something the world has never seen. Somewhere down the road, take a second, and tell your story to help someone else in this world.

MEET THE AUTHOR

Our author, Wallace J. Miles, had a dream when he was four-years-old, and that dream has helped define the path of his life thus far. He set out on a path to accomplish that dream even though no one believed it was for him. Wallace achieved academic excellence, excelled in sports, rose from walk-on kicker to a record-breaking college receiver, and earned the opportunity to compete in the NFL along the way. He earned his Electrical Engineering degree from the illustrious North Carolina A&T State University along the same way. Wallace played in the NFL and the CFL (Canadian Football League), where he won a Grey Cup Championship with the Edmonton Eskimos. Now, he has found success again in the construction industry, where he utilizes old skills as the foundation to achieve new dreams.